SPECTACULAR WINERIES
of Washington

Published by

SIGNATURE
PUBLISHING GROUP

1424 Gables Court
Plano, TX 75075
469.246.6060
Fax: 469.246.6062
www.panache.com

Publisher: Brian G. Carabet
Publisher: Jolie M. Carpenter

Printed in Canada

Distributed by Independent Publishers Group
800.888.4741

PUBLISHER'S DATA

Spectacular Wineries of Washington

Library of Congress Control Number: 2012930878

ISBN 13: 978-0-9832398-5-7
ISBN 10: 0-9832398-5-1

First Printing 2012

10 9 8 7 6 5 4 3 2 1

Right: Leonetti Cellar, page 142

Previous Page: Boushey Vineyards, page 276

SPECTACULAR WINERIES
of Washington

FOREWORD

When I first started running restaurants in Seattle, there were dominant forces that had to be acknowledged on our menus: briny Puget Sound oysters, plump steel-blue mussels from Penn Cove, sharp-clawed Dungeness crabs, deep-sea Alaskan halibut, and of course our many species of wild salmon. These were menu staples you wouldn't want to be caught without. However, every wine list in town was draped in wines from California and Europe—that's just the way it was. Well, not anymore!

Our fair state is now blessed with more than a thousand wineries, many of which are profiled in this magnificent book. Customers demanding local, sustainable produce recognize that a meal isn't all it could be unless it's paired with wines from the local terroir. Washington State vinifera grapes jump to attention when matched with San Juan Island lamb or beef fed on Ellensburg alfalfa. The snowy Cascade Range rivers irrigate thousands of acres of hops, apples, pears, peaches, mint, lentils, and most every grape varietal you can imagine.

My wife Jackie and I were so smitten with Washington wine country that we bought our own 20 acres, six of which supply our restaurants with organically grown herbs and vegetables. Next into the soil will be muscato grapes dedicated to making a classic, fizzy, aromatic dessert wine. Our hope is to have enough to share a sweet sip with every diner after dinner in our restaurants, as a parting and lasting memory of what Washington has to offer.

Cheers,

Tom Douglas

Chef, restaurateur, and author

Quilceda Creek Vintners, page 196

Willow Crest Winery 262

INTRODUCTION

Staking claim to a truly unique place in the world of wine, Washington State stands at the precipice of the modern American West—geographically, historically, and stylistically—and *Spectacular Wineries of Washington* proves a thought-provoking and visually delightful introduction to this burgeoning winemaking region.

The state comprises a mosaic of landscapes extending from lush evergreen-lined coasts in the west and towering snow-capped mountains in the center to a vast sagebrush-laden desert in the east, home to world-renowned vineyards.

Washington State's growing regions also lie in arguably one of the most ideal latitudes in the Northern Hemisphere, between the 46th and 47th parallels—identical to France's famed Bordeaux and Burgundy. This northerly position affords Washington State up to two hours more daylight at the height of its growing season compared to more southerly regions such as California.

Bisecting the state from north to south, the volcanic Cascade Mountains shield the eastern agricultural core from the maritime influence of the Pacific Ocean to the west, providing ample heat accumulation for optimal ripening of a multitude of classic vinifera varieties. Despite the desert heat, temperatures throughout this arid region shift dramatically from day to night—sometimes as much as 50 degrees Fahrenheit—preserving abundant natural acidity to balance the pure expression of varietal fruit character.

Leonetti Cellar, page 142

The Woodhouse Wine Estates, page 264

While the geography of Washington State has been forming since time immemorial, it was the cataclysmic Missoula Floods, a series of events originating in western Montana and sweeping across eastern Washington periodically at the end of the last ice age around 15,000 years ago, that left behind scores of dramatic bluffs and canyons and deposited an array of exotic soils not found anywhere else on the planet. This wonderfully distinct geology forms the literal foundation of Washington State wine.

Long Shadows Vintners, page 146

Corliss Estates Winery, page 98

The same amazing terrain that captivated early settlers more than 200 years ago remains today; modern explorers discover one of the world's most dynamic wine regions taking root among beautifully restored barns and farmhouses. Though steeped in the rich agricultural traditions of the region, the meteoric rise of the modern wine industry in Washington State is an astonishingly recent phenomenon.

Unlike California, Washington State's wine industry did not begin immediately with the repeal of Prohibition. While evidence of winemaking dates to the establishment of Fort Vancouver by the Hudson's Bay Company in the 1820s, it was not until the 1960s, when a group of professors and amateur winemakers from the University of Washington incorporated themselves, that dry varietal wines made from vinifera finally became commercially available.

Boudreaux Cellars, page 54

Stevens Winery, page 218

Northstar Winery, page 180

Once this seed was planted, it was not long before a thriving wine industry spread to all corners of the state. Today, Washington State boasts more than 43,000 acres of vineyards supplying more than 700 wineries, placing the state second in the country for total production. Yet the same spirit of exploration and innovation that inspired our early pioneers to first plant grapevines in Washington State still drives our contemporary grape growers and winemakers to create one of the most unique and diverse wine regions in the world.

This diversity springs from our varied soils and distinct geographical regions as well as the people from around the world who have come to Washington State to join our dynamic wine industry. Through their collective dedication to the expression of a distinct sense of place in every bottle, Washington State's wines have earned global recognition. And yet, for all of their critical and commercial success, Washington State's grape growers and winemakers have not lost their humility and collegiality. It is still common to enter a tasting room and be greeted with a firm handshake and a full glass by the winemaker himself.

Whether you are already a Washington State wine enthusiast or you are experiencing the region for the first time, we invite you to savor the unique story behind every bottle. Along the way to discovering several new favorites, we hope that you will also discover a few new friends.

Upland Vineyards, page 244

CONTENTS

Mercer Estates Winery, page 166

OFF THE VINE

"It is exciting to make artisan wines that are generating such recognition, proving once again Washington State is one of the great wine-producing regions in the world. —Rob Griffin, Barnard Griffin

Columbia Winery, page 94

L'Ecole Nº 41, page 138

Betz Family Winery, page 46

Sparkman Cellars, page 210

Waterbrook Winery, page 258

WINERIES

Alder Ridge Estate Winery

Prosser

A triple threat, Peter Devison of Alder Ridge Estate Winery is well-educated, well-traveled, and a well-seasoned winemaker. With a degree in kinesiology from Vancouver, the Nova Scotia native set off for New Zealand in pursuit of a second degree in enology. It was here—and in Australia—that he developed a preference for modern winemaking methods and state-of-the-art facilities. After relocating to Washington in 2004, he quickly became recognized as an industry all-star and was wooed to Alder Ridge in 2009.

Just 15 miles west of Patterson, Alder Ridge Vineyard is part of the Horse Heaven Hills appellation and overlooks the Columbia River from a height of 1,000 feet. A collection of small vineyard lots and larger estate rows grow over sheer, southern-facing slopes that vary in elevation. This makes for a vineyard of micro-climates, which offer diversified fruit and an abundant range of flavors.

Alder Ridge Estate Winery shares a space with Apex Cellars—whose wine is also crafted by Peter using Alder Ridge Vineyard grapes—called Apex at Alder Ridge in Woodinville's amiable tasting district. Here wine lovers can taste an acclaimed Alder Ridge Estate cabernet sauvignon or one of the many well-received wines that Apex has to offer.

Top: Winemaker Peter Devison.

Bottom: Cabernet sauvignon grapes three weeks prior to harvest.

Facing page: Peter Devison assessing the Alder Ridge vineyard with the Columbia River in the background.
Photographs by Andréa Johnson

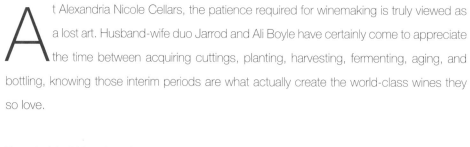

Alexandria Nicole Cellars

Prosser

At Alexandria Nicole Cellars, the patience required for winemaking is truly viewed as a lost art. Husband-wife duo Jarrod and Ali Boyle have certainly come to appreciate the time between acquiring cuttings, planting, harvesting, fermenting, aging, and bottling, knowing those interim periods are what actually create the world-class wines they so love.

Founded in 2004, the winery wasn't part of Jarrod and Ali's original plans. In fact, a piece of barren land on Horse Heaven Hills provided the inspiration that started it all. Jarrod was a viticulturalist and grower relations liaison at Hogue Cellars with a strong passion for winemaking, and when he saw the unbroken land it was love at first sight. Providence led Jarrod and Ali to partner with the Mercer family who owned the land, and together they created Destiny Ridge Vineyard in 1998. While the initial vision called for the fruit to be used for small case lots for other wineries, the grapes had such amazing quality that they inspired their own winery.

Named after Ali, Alexandria Nicole Cellars crafts more than two dozen varieties of elegant but approachable wines. Just as the story for the winery started with the great vineyard location, so do the wines themselves. Jarrod likes to say that it is "all about the dirt," and although Destiny Ridge Vineyard is able to support production of around 70,000 cases a year on its 265 acres, Jarrod has purposefully maintained boutique winery production levels. This allows him to focus on crafting wines that showcase the terroir of the vineyard. The same passion that sparked the winery's inception continues today, as evidenced by the award-winning wines and 2011 Washington Winery of the Year award from *Wine Press Northwest*.

Top: The large metal sign that hangs on the barrel room door was crafted by vineyard foreman José Yanez and Seph Boyle.
Photograph by Andréa Johnson

Middle: The Boyle family at their estate vineyard: Seph, Matti, Jarrod, Ali and Kol all enjoy being involved in the family business.
Photograph by Sunny Wright, courtesy of Alexandria Nicole Cellars

Bottom: A sampling of Alexandria Nicole's award-winning wines.
Photograph by Andréa Johnson

Facing page: Destiny Ridge Vineyard, located in the Horse Heaven Hills.
Photograph by Andréa Johnson

Amavi Cellars

Walla Walla

Inspired by the Latin words *amor, vita,* and *vinum*—meaning love, life, and wine—the founders of Amavi Cellars blended three terms into one of phonetic beauty. A sister property of Pepper Bridge Winery, which is known for its Bordeaux varietals, Amavi specializes in cabernet sauvignon, sémillon, and syrah. Following in the footsteps of Ray Goff and Norm McKibben, second-generation partners Travis Goff and Eric McKibben apply a fresh approach to the family tradition.

Winemaker, viticulturist, and partner Jean-François grew up with an intimate perspective of vineyards. Working alongside his father in Rolle, Switzerland, Jean-François developed the same passion and respect for the art that his father and grandfather possessed. Once old enough to choose his own path, he earned degrees in viticulture and winemaking and moved on to make wine and manage vineyards in Switzerland, Spain, and California before establishing himself in Washington.

Three estate vineyards contribute fruit for the production of Amavi's wines. Covering 600 acres of the Walla Walla Valley appellation, Seven Hills, Pepper Bridge, and Les Collines Vineyards are all certified sustainable by Salmon-Safe and the International Organization for Biological Control. The Valley is blessed with rich loess soils from ancient glacial floods and volcanic minerals delivered by ash-spewing eruptions from Washington's Mount St. Helens and Oregon's Mount Mazama. World-class cabernet sauvignon, merlot, cabernet franc, malbec, sémillon, and syrah thrive in Amavi's three estate vineyards.

Top: Amavi Cellars partner Travis Goff, tasting room manager Patty Lynch, and partner Eric McKibben.

Bottom: Beautiful vines growing in the estate vineyard adjacent to Amavi.

Facing page: Enjoy Amavi wines and spectacular views of the Blue Mountains and estate vineyards from the spacious tasting room deck.
Photographs by Andréa Johnson

Seated within acres of verdant vineyards, the winery is a modern structure comprised of stained wood, steel, and a profusion of glass. The geometrical gem, designed by esteemed Seattle architect David Clinkston, is a vision of clean, angular lines. The winery's sharp features contrast with, yet complement, the soft rolling foothills of the neighboring Blue Mountains. A stunning 20-foot zinc bar encourages patrons to mingle while spectacular views of the vineyards and surrounding terrain can be admired from the large glass wall or outside on the inviting deck.

Above: Adjacent to the tasting room, the gallery room is available for winemaker dinners, luncheons, wedding receptions, and business meetings.

Left: Enjoy the open, Zen-like serenity of the tasting room.

Facing page: The tasting room is surrounded by the lush estate vineyard.
Photographs by Andréa Johnson

WINE & FARE

Syrah
Pair with slow-cooked lamb chops over risotto
and red peppers sautéed in lamb stock.

Sémillon
Couple with pan-seared scallops over angel hair pasta
in butter-cream sauce.

Cabernet Sauvignon
Sip with Kobe beef stew complete with sweet onions,
red potatoes, carrots, and tomatoes.

Tastings
Open to the public daily, year-round
Also available at Woodinville tasting room

Watch a video of Travis Goff and Eric McKibben
discussing Amavi's neoteric tasting room, situated
within one of the estate's three flourishing vineyards.

Amavi Cellars

AMOR · VITA · VINUM

Apex Cellars

Prosser

pex—meaning summit, zenith, or climax—acutely indicates the goal of Apex Cellars, which is to produce the best reserve-style wine within a price range affordable enough for consumers to enjoy daily. With numerous bottles receiving 90-plus points from notable publications and making best buy and value wine lists each year, the limited vintages are subject to selling out, leaving consumers wanting more.

Due to Peter Devison signing on as Apex Cellars' lead winemaker in 2009, loyal followers are sure to notice subtle enhancements to classics such as chardonnay, cabernet sauvignon, and merlot. While studying enology and viticulture at New Zealand's Lincoln University, Peter became exposed to high-caliber wineries functioning with the best technologies and latest designs. This exposure led to his preference for working in winemaking facilities using energy-efficient features, something Apex also appreciates.

The tasting room, located in the Winemaker's Loft in Prosser, has a vast selection to sample from. Visitors can uncork an Apex Cellars exclusive or peruse a collection of sister winery gems to enjoy.

Top: Apex Cellars' tasting room.
Photograph courtesy of Apex Cellars

Bottom: Apex Cellars' chardonnay.
Photograph courtesy of Apex Cellars

Facing page: Columbia Valley cabernet sauvignon.
Photograph by Andréa Johnson

Arbor Crest Wine Cellars

Spokane

I n the late 1970s, three family members set out to attain for Spokane, Washington, the same success the California wine country was enjoying. The endeavor has paid off, and today Arbor Crest Wine Cellars produces some of Washington's top wines: quality vintages that speak to terroir and family tradition.

Extensive tasting had led brothers David and Harry Mielke, as well as Harry's wife Marcia, to believe that Washington could be the next great wine state. After a UC Davis education and an experimental vineyard, the Mielkes decided to found a winery in Spokane and source grapes from what would be the Columbia Valley appellation. Choosing a name proved a challenge, but after one long night of deliberation the family selected Arbor Crest Wine Cellars in order to be at the top of the list. In 1982, soon after purchasing a California winery and moving its operations to the family's old cherry-packing facility in Spokane, Arbor Crest released its first wine—a sauvignon blanc made from Bacchus Vineyard grapes. The winery's focus on bringing out the flavor of the grapes in the vineyard has been steadfast since the beginning.

Now that Arbor Crest had made its debut as the 29th Washington winery, it needed a spectacular tasting room location. Enter the Royal Riblet estate, a Spokane Valley National Historic Landmark dating to the 1920s. The Mielke family took ownership of the three-story Florentine mansion in 1984. Now known as the Cliff House Estate due to its location atop a 450-foot basalt rock face, the mansion offers unparalleled views of the city and landscape. The chance to combine superb wines with beautiful views proved irresistible to the people of Spokane, and today the estate regularly hosts concerts, weddings, private events, and community fundraisers.

Top: Owners Marcia and Harold Mielke started Arbor Crest in 1982 as the 29th winery in the state.
Photograph by Kristina Mielke-van Löben Sels

Bottom: Second-generation owners Kristina and Jim van Löben Sels proudly stand below the Cliff House in Arbor Crest's five-acre estate vineyard.
Photograph by Andréa Johnson

Facing page: The Arbor Crest Cliff House, built in 1924, is perched on the edge of a 450-foot cliff with panoramic views of the Spokane area.
Photograph by Don Hamilton

In 1999, everything came full circle when Harry and Marcia's daughter Kristina Mielke-van Löben Sels and her husband Jim took over Arbor Crest as winemaker and vineyard manager, respectively. Graduates of UC Davis, Kristina and Jim make an excellent team: she relies on him to achieve the best concentration and balance in the fruit by working closely with the growers at the source vineyards in the Columbia Valley, Wahluke Slope, and Red Mountain appellations. Kristina can then focus on crafting ultra-premium wines by taking a minimalist approach that captures the power of the fruit. Arbor Crest's wines that pair easily with food and possess a natural integrity to terroir include particular specialties of sauvignon blanc, chardonnay, cabernet sauvignon, cabernet franc, sangiovese, and syrah. The result is delicious wines across the board, making it clear why *Wine Spectator* named the winery one of the Top 50 Wine Producers Everyone Should Know in 2004.

Top: Jim van Löben Sels and son Carl play a game of checkers on the historic giant checkerboard at Arbor Crest.
Photograph by Andréa Johnson

Middle: Winemaker and owner Kristina Mielke-van Löben Sels draws a sample of fermenting cabernet sauvignon juice from a tank during harvest.
Photograph by Andréa Johnson

Bottom: Arbor Crest Estate's beautiful arched gatehouse, originally built as a guest house, is now home to several offices.
Photograph by Carlton Canary

Facing page: An overview of the spectacular grounds at the estate offers views of the giant checkerboard, the swimming pool, and lush foliage.
Photograph by Andréa Johnson

WINE & FARE

Wahluke Slope Vineyard Sangiovese
Pair with corned beef.

Conner Lee Vineyard Chardonnay
Serve with crab quiche.

Dionysus
(cabernet sauvignon, merlot, cabernet franc, malbec, petit verdot)
Pair with braised short ribs.

Tastings
Open to the public daily, year-round
Also available at River Park Square Tasting Room, Spokane

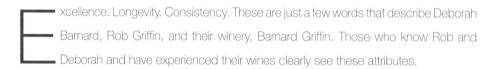

Barnard Griffin
Richland

E xcellence. Longevity. Consistency. These are just a few words that describe Deborah Barnard, Rob Griffin, and their winery, Barnard Griffin. Those who know Rob and Deborah and have experienced their wines clearly see these attributes.

Deborah and Rob met in college at the University of California, Davis, where Rob completed a degree in enology. Despite his professor's advice to the contrary, Rob felt that Washington State was an up-and-coming wine region and, because of this, he moved to Richland in 1977.

Rob and Deborah are truly pioneers of the Washington wine scene, having fostered the industry's reputation and helped to cultivate the state into the second-largest wine producer in America. Rob, who was named the 2010 honorary vintner for the prestigious Auction of Washington Wines, has been making wine on a continuous basis longer than any other Washington State winemaker.

Once established in Washington, Rob and Deborah got to work on their own creation, developing the Barnard Griffin label in 1983 and opening the Richland winery in 1996.

Barnard Griffin has received heavy praise for many of its wines, and it continues to demonstrate leadership in the Washington wine industry. Rob Griffin says, "It is exciting to make artisan wines that are generating such recognition, proving once again Washington State is one of the great wine-producing regions in the world."

Top: Owners Rob Griffin and Deborah Barnard, in their Richland tasting room, are Washington State wine pioneers.
Photograph by Andréa Johnson

Bottom: Perfect at room temperature or on ice, Barnard Griffin's rosé of sangiovese has won gold or better at the San Francisco Chronicle Wine Competition—seven years in a row!
Photograph by Elise Barnard Griffin

Facing page: The Barnard Griffin Winery tower looms behind the basalt entrance sign with fused glass addition, created by glass artist and winery co-owner Deborah Barnard.
Photograph by Andréa Johnson

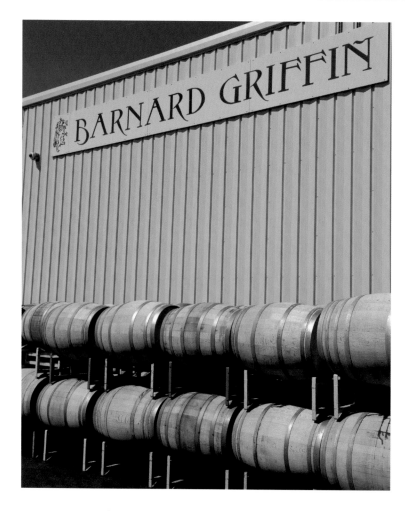

The winery produces two labels, both available through retail stores, wine clubs, and online wine venues. The Reserve Label wines are crafted in limited quantities from the best vineyard lots in the region, using European and American oak. Barnard Griffin's signature Tulip Label wine, available across the nation, is a mainstay on many restaurant lists and dinner tables, and it is one of the state's most recognized brands.

Cabernet sauvignon and merlot are two varietals for which Barnard Griffin has a reputation for excellence. In 2011, the merlot was named one of the top 100 wines by the San Francisco Chronicle as well as the best merlot at the Washington State Wine Competition. In that same competition, the largest professionally judged wine tasting in Washington, the cabernet sauvignon won best red, an award the wine has received several years in a row.

Rob's longevity in the industry has cultivated a deep knowledge, understanding, and appreciation for the growing areas of the state and the complexity that the terroirs bring to the wine. This intimate knowledge gives Rob the best perspective and guides his savvy sourcing and selection of fruit.

As Washington State's premier family-owned winery, Barnard Griffin is moving into its middle age with the help of Rob and Deborah's daughters, Elise and Megan Barnard Griffin. Elise is taking advantage of her business marketing degree, while Megan is applying her enology degree by refining her knowledge of the art of wine alchemy with the help of her father.

The Richland winery also features an expanded tasting room and an enhanced glass studio. These are in addition to a 2010-built barrel room, as well as a landscaped gazebo on a berm overlooking the confluence of the Yakima and Columbia rivers.

Visiting the tasting room and fused glass studio gives an amazing look at the artistry that goes into making each and every bottle of wine. Barnard Griffin is an important stop on any tour of Washington's best wineries.

Left: French and American oak barrels filled with Barnard Griffin merlot from the Columbia Valley AVA and racked just outside the Richland winery.

Right: Two generations of Barnard Griffin winemakers: Assistant winemaker Megan Griffin and owner and winemaker Rob Griffin pose in front of winery's massive oak vats containing cabernet sauvignon and syrah.

Facing page: Rob Griffin works with many vineyards throughout the Columbia Valley, including the Gunkel Vineyard at the Maryhill site.
Photographs by Andréa Johnson

Cabernet Sauvignon
Pair with any dish or meat that calls for a concentrated, richly textured wine.

Chardonnay
Excellent with nearly anything, including poultry, pasta, and even shellfish.

Malbec
Outstanding with rich, tomato-sauced dishes and spicy foods.

Tastings
Open daily, year-round

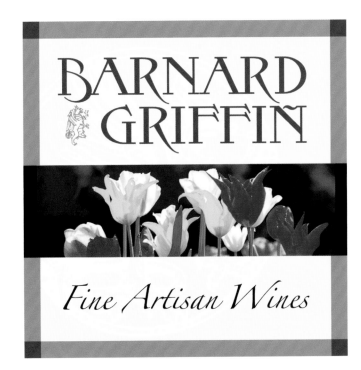

BARNARD GRIFFIN

Fine Artisan Wines

Basel Cellars
Estate Winery

Walla Walla

At first glance, the 87-acre estate appears to be of national park caliber, stretching across the Blue Mountain foothills and overlooking the vast Walla Walla Valley. At second glance, 27 acres of planted vineyard are spotted, and the true purpose of Basel Cellars Estate Winery is revealed. A lodge and winery, the former residence is equipped to host weddings and receptions, corporate functions, family reunions, and many other hospitable events on the grounds. A small situation of large-scale buildings surrounded by impressive landscaping, a sparkling pool, and rows of lush grape leaves invites guests to explore the grounds and capture unparalleled views of the valley while sipping a famous estate blend.

The well-respected source of cabernet, cabernet franc, merlot, malbec, and syrah presented its first official bottle of wine in 2001 and has since received well-deserved attention from *Wine Enthusiast* and *Wines & Spirits* magazines for a number of vintages and varietals. The namesakes of the estate, Greg and Becky Basel, opened the winery in 2002 and invited newcomers Steve and Jo Marie Hansen to become business partners in 2004. Since then the Hansens have grown into majority owners of the estate and are responsible for its current success. The majority of their fruit comes from 35-acre Pheasant Run Vineyard—planted in 1997 by Greg and Becky—and 26-acre Double River Vineyard, which is viewable from the tasting room's fantastic patio.

Top: The turret and main office of the winery.

Bottom: Grapes ripening on the vine.

Facing page: The grand entrance to the estate.
Photographs by Andréa Johnson

The main building of the estate—designed to mirror other great American lodges such as Yosemite's Awahnee Hotel, Mary Colter's Bright Angel Lodge, and Mt. Hood's Timberline Lodge—is perched on the pinnacle of the property, boasting the best views of both the valley and mountains. Understated opulence is in no shortage at the lodge and is found throughout the eight rooms, cabana house, gourmet kitchen, dining rooms, and downstairs game room. Details such as hand-carved red cedar wood doors, hanging antler chandeliers, and a Harley Davidson room invite guests to explore both the indoors and out.

Left: The tasting room and entrance's Old World style.

Facing page: Lush foliage overlooking the spacious valley.
Photographs by Andréa Johnson

WINE & FARE

Merlot
Pair with filet mignon seared in garlic butter with sautéed mushrooms and fresh spinach.

Cabernet
Pair with roasted duck wrapped in applewood smoked bacon with baked rosemary new potatoes.

Syrah
Pair with artisan pizza topped with mozzarella cheese, Roma tomatoes, and fresh basil.

Tastings
Open to public, year-round

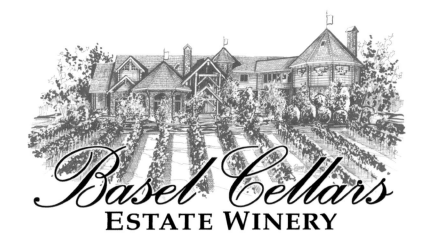

Basel Cellars
ESTATE WINERY

Benson Vineyards Estate Winery

Manson

The beautiful, glacier-fed Lake Chelan is a scenic backdrop for Benson Vineyards Estate Winery—one of the few 100 percent estate-grown wineries in the area. The family-owned operation first became an idea in 1995, after Paul and Kathy Benson spent many a vacation in wine-producing areas on the West Coast. When Paul retired in 1996, the couple chose to turn their vacation cottage into their current residence and spent nearly two years familiarizing themselves with the art of grape growing and winemaking.

By 2000, they'd officially broken ground and recruited the full-time aid of their two sons, Scott and Jeff, to establish Benson Vineyards. First they removed the existing apple orchard and prepped the land for planting. Two years later, Benson Vineyards had 23 acres of vineyards to its name, accounting for 10 vinifera grape varieties. Another two years later, and the Benson family reaped their first harvest. Today they produce 11 varietals, including seven reds and four whites, resulting in 5,000 finished cases each year. The warm north shore of Lake Chelan and the south-facing vineyards are strategic to maximizing summer heat for ripening the red grapes to perfection. These include syrah, pinot noir, nebbiolo, cabernet franc, cabernet sauvignon, sangiovese, and merlot. Benson's white varietals feature viognier, pinot gris, chardonnay, and gewürztraminer.

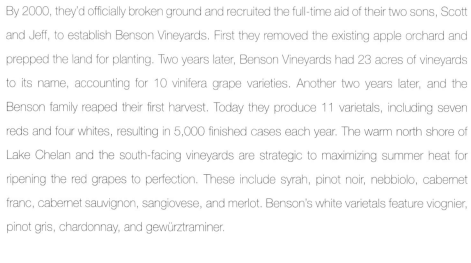

Top: Benson's Mediterranean-style tasting room and dining area overlook the beautiful vineyards and Lake Chelan.

Bottom: The entrance to Benson's modern and inviting tasting room.

Facing page: View from Benson's tasting room deck of the rolling vineyard, Lake Chelan, and Stormy Mountain.
Photographs by Andrèa Johnson

The Bensons pride themselves on treating their wine with individual care and attention, overseeing the process from vineyard to the tasting room. By owning and controlling each and every vineyard used in the production of the wines, they offer a unique depth of quality and passion for excellent winemaking. A Benson Vineyards signature is viognier—its floral notes expound upon hints of pineapple and stone fruits—which is also available in an icewine style made from frozen grapes to produce a sweet, concentrated palate of peach, apricot, pear, caramel apple, and butterscotch. Visitors have quickly identified the sangiovese as one of the vineyard's top red wines, with bing cherry, clove, and herb flavors. The red blends are also a draw, featuring bold and balanced tannins.

A casual Mediterranean-themed tasting room and headquarters warmly welcomes wine enthusiasts and traveling passersby for monthly wine dinners, mid-week afternoon music events, and seasonal celebrations. The Benson family also offers wedding and event hosting for unique occasions spent basking in the glow of a fiery sunset amid captivating views of the lakeside, rows of pristine vineyards, and a rolling, hilly landscape.

Top: Harvest activity at Benson Vineyards.

Middle: Paul Benson delivering recently hand-picked grapes to the winery for processing.

Bottom: Paul Benson and winemaker Scott Benson examining just-harvested viognier grapes.

Facing page: Winery guests relaxing and enjoying their favorite wines while taking in the beautiful views of the vineyards and Lake Chelan.
Photographs by Andréa Johnson

Estate Viognier
Superb with summer appetizers, fresh fruit, cheeses, and shellfish.

Estate Pinot Gris
Perfectly pairs with curry chicken, lime and cilantro zesty pork, or Thai food.

Estate Sangiovese
Wonderful with fresh Italian tomato dishes and classic caprese salads.

Estate Syrah
Delicious with grilled meats of all kinds, such as roasted pork, barbecue, and stews.

Tastings
Open to the public daily, year-round

Beresan Winery

Walla Walla

The essence of family-owned Beresan Winery—founded in 2001 by Thomas Waliser and now joined by wife Debbie and their sons Tim and Scott—is expressed through its location in a restored, turn-of-the-century barn and outer building; both speak to award-winning wines that are rooted in the past but cognizant of the future. The two-story barn, originally part of the Thomas homestead, is well known by locals whose fathers and grandfathers broke in their horses there. The winery's name also speaks to the past, originating from the Ukrainian region where the Walisers settled in the early 1800s.

Thomas, who grew up in Walla Walla Valley, was a respected horticultural apple consultant for 15 years before he began his foray into wine grapes by farming Pepper Bridge Vineyards and Seven Hills West Vineyards. Designated by the Washington Association of Wine Grape Growers and *Wine & Spirits* magazine as the grower of the year in 2008 and 2009, respectively, it's clear that Thomas knows viticulture.

Born and raised on Bainbridge Island, winemaker Thomas Glase moved to Walla Walla and worked as assistant winemaker at L'Ecole N° 41 before joining with Beresan. His philosophy of crafting wines that express the unique character of the vineyard pairs nicely with Beresan's goals.

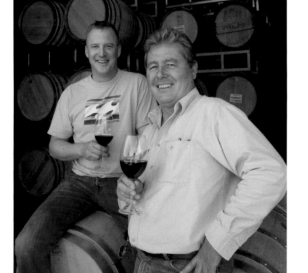

Naturally, the focus at Beresan is on the estate vineyards: Waliser Vineyard, Yellow Jacket Vineyard, and Beresan Estate Vineyard. While unique, they all have in common cobblestone soil and certifications for sustainability. Red varietals include cabernet sauvignon, merlot, cabernet franc, and syrah, from which the winery blends several red wines, and carménère and malbec to stand on their own. Sémillon and riesling are the white varietals.

Top: The entryway to the winery's tasting room.
Photograph by Andréa Johnson

Bottom: The "two Toms" that define Beresan Winery: winemaker Tom Glase and owner and vineyard grower Tom Waliser.
Photograph by Alexei Kazantsev

Facing page: Established in 2001 inside two renovated barns, Beresan Winery is nestled in the middle of one of its three estate vineyards in Walla Walla.
Photograph by Tom Walsier

Betz Family Winery

Woodinville

C all it a fortunate coincidence. Call it luck. But if you ask Steve Griessel, he'll tell you without hesitation that in 2010, "synchronicity" led him and his wife Bridgit to Betz Family Winery. Located in Woodinville, Betz Family Winery has operated as a limited-production, award-winning winery since 1997.

Though the Betz Family Winery crushed its first grapes in the late '90s, winery founder Bob Betz was far from a stranger to the art and science of winemaking. For the better part of four decades, Bob and his wife Cathy have pursued a global knowledge of wine, culled from their travels and training in France, Germany, and Italy in the early 1970s. It is with this valued international perspective that Bob began working for Chateau Ste. Michelle in 1976, where he was eventually appointed vice president of winemaking research. He earned a Master of Wine degree in 1998.

Throughout the following years, Bob fine-tuned a comprehensive understanding of the terroir of Columbia Valley vineyards and how growing conditions of various sites determine the unique character of the wines they make, each with its distinct flavors and intensity. Over the years, the Betz Family Winery has built trusted partnerships with top Washington vineyards, managed by smart, intuitive winegrowers. These relationships lead to shared values and a commitment to growing the best fruit possible for Betz wines. This philosophy demands keen observation, a high work ethic, and constant attention to detail from both grower and winemaker. With his global perspective, Betz considers Washington's Columbia Valley one of the world's most blessed sites to grow classic wine grapes, with a unique combination of climate, soil, and geography that creates world-class grapes. And wine lovers agree: Consider the staggering fact that in just one decade, Washington wineries have increased 400 percent, making it the second-highest wine-producing state in the country.

Top: The Columbia Valley's unique combination of climate, soil, and geography creates world-class grapes. Betz Family Winery works with selected growers in specific vineyards to nurture the very best the sites can produce.

Bottom: Since 1997, Betz Family Winery has produced a range of award-winning reds based on Rhône and Bordeaux varieties.

Facing page: Boushey Vineyards is the source for one of the Betz Family's most acclaimed syrahs, La Serenne.
Photographs by Steve Griessel

While a deal was struck between Betz and the Griessels to purchase the winery, a partnership was also formed. Steve and Bridgit have vowed to maintain the integrity of the vineyard and winery by partnering with Bob to serve as winemaker for the indefinite future, producing an enviable variety of Bordeaux and Rhône-inspired wines. Betz Family Winery will remain a small family winery enveloped in all the ideals that have made it renowned since 1997. Both Steve and Bob are committed to impeccable professional character and practices, with constant quality improvement. And at the core, they know nothing happens by chance.

Since that first Betz Family Winery vintage of 150 cases, Bob has successfully produced award-winning wines and helped put Washington on the map as a world-class contender; it is with this grounding responsibility that Steve and Bridgit now take the helm. The practices and actions of everyone involved with the Betz winery remain true to the core beliefs and spirit on which it was founded and continue into the next chapter of the Betz Family Winery story.

Above left: A partnership for the future, founders Bob and Cathy Betz and owners Bridgit and Steve Griessel share the values and philosophy that family can bring to a limited-production winery.
Photograph by Andréa Johnson

Top: Bob Betz leads the team through a series of blending trials over several weeks until the wine reflects the character of the vintage and terroir and is in perfect balance.
Photograph by Andréa Johnson

Bottom: The winery was opened in time for the 2005 harvest; beauty and functionality was the quest.
Photograph by Steve Griessel

Facing page: Not just a winery but a labor of love, the winery is home to family events on the bocce court or animated lunches and tastings under the pergola.
Photograph by Steve Griessel

WINE & FARE

Besoleil
Ideal with wood-fired grilled salmon or any grilled meat.

Clos de Betz
Perfect with roasted duck with black cherry glaze.

Cabernet Sauvignon Père de Famille
Amazing with roasted lamb marinated in rosemary, thyme, and oregano-scented sauce.

Syrah La Serenne
Wonderful with a classic layered lasagna or gourmet pizza.

Tastings
Closed to the public

Watch a video of Betz Family Winery owner Steve Griessel and founder and winemaker Bob Betz explaining why the Washington terroir is a vital element in producing incredible wine.

BETZ
FAMILY WINERY

1997

Bookwalter Winery

Richland

It may be a simple adage, but for John Bookwalter at Bookwalter Winery, great wines are grown in the vineyard. Following each grape varietal from the vineyard through the winemaking process, John develops wine based on the specific varietal and needs of the grape. From there, the flavors are captured to result in great, ultra-premium Washington wines.

Bookwalter Winery is located in the heart of the Washington wine country, producing small lots of reds and whites, each of which offers the perfect marriage of vibrant local geology and a long agricultural history of the Bookwalter family, which dates back to the 18th century in Europe. Grape growing pioneer Jerry Bookwalter produced his first wines in 1983—a chardonnay, a chenin blanc, and a Johannisberg riesling—and within another year he'd already expanded into reds.

Soon Jerry's wife, Jean, took charge of operations, and the couple worked through the inaugural years of the Washington wine industry, shaping the future along the way. A decade later, John—the Bookwalters' son who had spent nearly a decade in beverage sales and marketing—joined the team. The family's long legacy in the industry enabled John, who now leads the winery, to craft the best possible wines from grapes harvested from Washington's most established vineyards, those which have a proven depth of flavor.

Top: JBistro features small plates of chef-inspired local cuisine.
Photograph by Andréa Johnson

Bottom: A collection of J. Bookwalter Second Edition wines: Conflict, Protagonist, and Chapter 2.
Photograph courtesy of J. Bookwalter

Facing page: A stately old birch tree provides shade over the front gardens, dining area, and patio at Bookwalter Winery.
Photograph by Andréa Johnson

Alongside the family's expertise, John enlisted famed Napa Valley winemaker Zelma Long and world-renowned winemaking consultant Claude Gros to further enhance the winery's evolution, while creating a lasting impression on Bookwalter's distinct wine style developed in concert with these successful wine industry icons.

Premium grape sources set the bar high for wines that are ripe, lush, balanced, and complex. Bookwalter white wines are dynamic, fermented and aged in stainless tanks to maintain a sense of place and clarity. The reds are aged exclusively in French oak barrels and succeed in providing vibrant, rich, and deeply satisfying flavors right away.

Delightfully bookish in name—Protagonist, Conflict, and Foreshadow, to name a few—the wines have pulled in rave reviews since the beginning. John's dedication and passion have shot the winery to the top of lists by everyone from *Wine Enthusiast* to Robert Parker. *Wine Press Northwest* named Bookwalter the winery of the year and *Sunset* magazine named Bookwalter the tasting room of the year. Accolades aside, Bookwalter's goal is to produce nothing less than wine that stands among the best in the world.

Top: The view over J. Bookwalter Vineyards and the bocce courts.

Bottom: Guests enjoy the bocce courts.

Facing page: The lower pergola and dining area in the gardens at Bookwalter Winery.
Photographs by Andréa Johnson

WINE & FARE

Conflict
Pair with great friends.

Antagonist
Perfect with game or foul.

Protagonist
Excellent with prime rib.

Chapter
Wonderful with anything decadent.

Tastings
Open to the public daily, year-round
Also available at J. Bookwalter Tasting Studio, Woodinville

Boudreaux Cellars
Leavenworth

oudreaux Cellars is a spectacular self-powered winery in the gorgeous Icicle Canyon eight miles outside Leavenworth. Its history is grounded in the legend of Boudreaux, that Cajun folklore character known for his brilliant sense of humor and relentless pursuit of high adventure. Louisiana native Rob Newsom was nicknamed Boudreaux by his winemaker friend, Gary Figgins, in the early 1990s. When Rob produced his first wine in 1998, Gary's son Chris dubbed it "The Cru Boudreaux." The Boudreaux Cellars name was impossible to avoid by the time the first commercial vintage was crushed in 2001. In a rare location, sourcing grapes from the oldest and best Washington State vineyards, utilizing the best barrels in the world, the winery began making waves on the national wine scene.

Renaissance man Rob—previously a professional alpinist and guide—gleaned wine knowledge from his friendships with Gary and Chris of Leonetti Cellar and Abeja Winery's John Abbott. Rob recalls his first piece of sincere advice from Gary as, "Aw, there's nothing to it. Just squash some grapes in a trash can and try to leave them alone." Eventually he did just that: the first wine, a merlot–cabernet franc blend, co-fermented outdoors on the porch over a propane camping stove! It aged in a new French oak barrel in the tiny cellar under his home, resulting in only twelve cases of a quality that spoke for itself.

Top: Assistant winemaker Tyler Vickrey lowers new barrels into the cellar.

Bottom: Tyler hand-punches fermenting bins of cabernet every eight hours for two weeks.

Facing page: Boudreaux Cellars is surrounded by fall color in Icicle Canyon in October.
Photographs by Andréa Johnson

Boudreaux Cellars is focused on cabernet sauvignon, crafted indoors now, and aged underground in a 230-barrel cellar. The building consists of local granite, laid by Rob and assistant winemaker Tyler Vickrey, and is filled with 2,000-gallon French oak tanks. The secluded winery's construction utilizes nature: gravity enables the wine to travel from the big wood hand-press to barrel, where it ages in the cellar's even, natural temperature. While the property has an experimental pinot noir vineyard, Rob sources grapes from the most complex blocks in Washington.

As a winemaker, Rob relies on techniques picked up from his mentors as well as his own intuition and awareness of the earth and sky learned from years of living outdoors as a climber and guide. A serious chef, he approaches winemaking from the perspective of a gourmand. Winemaking at Boudreaux is all about creativity, confidence, and problem solving. No Boudreaux wine has ever scored lower than 90 points in Robert Parker's *Wine Advocate*.

Rob's wife, Tamara, and daughter Keely—married to amateur vintner Jon McLain—round out the Boudreaux Cellars team. As at most small wineries, the family assists in winemaking, cleaning, bottling, sales, and marketing. Boudreaux wines are made with passion and meant to be shared as part of the beauty of life.

Top: Winemaker Rob Newsom hand-presses on the original Leonetti basket press.

Bottom: A small batch of Celilo Vineyard chardonnay is loaded into the press.

Facing page: The Boudreaux Cellars family—Jon McLain, Keely Newsom McLain, Tyler Vickrey, Tamara Newsom, and Rob Newsom—relaxes outside the winery.
Photographs by PatrickBennett.com

WINE & FARE

Reserve Cabernet Sauvignon
A meal by itself.

Cabernet Sauvignon
(cabernet sauvignon, cabernet franc, merlot, petit verdot)
Eminently suited for pairing with an aged ribeye steak.

Merlot
Pair with chicken-fried steak, potatoes, and brown gravy.

JBO's Frangio
(cabernet franc, sangiovese)
Pair with shrimp and grits, fresh pesto, or crab salad.

Tastings
Available at Boudreaux's Tasting Room, Leavenworth, and The Library, Woodinville
Winery open by appointment only, year-round

Watch a video of Rob Newsom playing his guitar and
discussing the history of Boudreaux Cellars.

Boudreaux
CELLARS

2007
CABERNET SAUVIGNON

CHAMPOUX AND LOESS VINEYARDS
WASHINGTON STATE

RESERVE

ROB NEWSOM
VINTNER

Brian Carter Cellars
Woodinville

Patriarch. Icon. Constant star. Washington winemakers have long used these words to refer to Brian Carter of Brian Carter Cellars. Since his first Washington vintage in 1980, Brian's influence has helped propel the state's wine industry from virtual obscurity to an international presence, which it deservedly commands. His involvement as winemaker, consultant, and guide to dozens of wineries has helped elevate Washington wines from regional industry to international powerhouse. Among Brian's many accomplishments, he is the only three-time recipient of the Pacific Northwest Enological Society's Grand Prize.

Passionate about blends, Brian is both a chemist and an artist who is known for producing exquisitely complex blended wines based on varietals such as cabernet sauvignon, merlot, grenache, sangiovese, tempranillo, and viognier. These become Solesce, Le Coursier, Byzance, Tuttorosso, Corrida, and Oriana, respectively. Solesce in particular, Brian's flagship blend, is painstakingly crafted using all five classic Bordeaux varieties, resulting in a wine both smooth and complex that boasts tones of blackberry, leather, toasted cedar, and cassis.

In 2006, Brian and his partner Mike Stevens opened the "little yellow tasting room," a remodeled garden home situated within the Hollywood area of Woodinville's wine country. The warm and quaint atmosphere reflects Brian's approach to wine: heartfelt and genuine. Guests with eager palates are welcomed by an enthusiastic staff and are encouraged to comfortably explore a collection of superb wines that reflect Brian's supreme passion for the art of blending.

Top: Brian enjoys a glass of his own making on the deck at Brian Carter Cellars' tasting room.

Middle: Steering whole clusters directly to the press, Brian is involved in almost every aspect of the operation—mind, body, and spirit.

Bottom: Blending is the ultimate art of winemaking, and it just happens to be the part that Brian enjoys the most.

Facing page: Guests sip wine outside Brian Carter's tasting room in Woodinville.
Photographs by Andréa Johnson

The Bunnell Family Cellar

Prosser

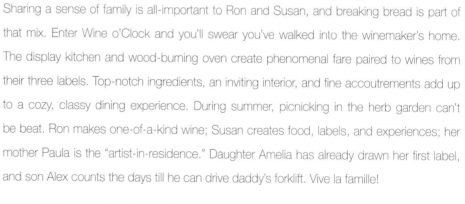

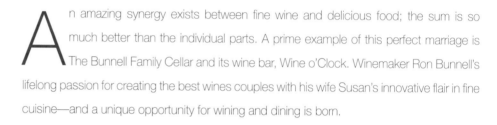

An amazing synergy exists between fine wine and delicious food; the sum is so much better than the individual parts. A prime example of this perfect marriage is The Bunnell Family Cellar and its wine bar, Wine o'Clock. Winemaker Ron Bunnell's lifelong passion for creating the best wines couples with his wife Susan's innovative flair in fine cuisine—and a unique opportunity for wining and dining is born.

A career spanning 30 years has shown Ron the importance of being a good steward of the wine, letting it speak for itself. The Bunnells' move to Washington launched their exploration of the developing region's unique viticultural possibilities, quickly convincing them the Columbia Valley was a natural home for traditional Rhône grapes. Ron now works with these and other varietals, grown by the top producers in the state, to produce exceptional varietal bottlings and blends. Handmade small lots of 50 to 250 cases equal purple palms for all the Bunnells every harvest.

Sharing a sense of family is all-important to Ron and Susan, and breaking bread is part of that mix. Enter Wine o'Clock and you'll swear you've walked into the winemaker's home. The display kitchen and wood-burning oven create phenomenal fare paired to wines from their three labels. Top-notch ingredients, an inviting interior, and fine accoutrements add up to a cozy, classy dining experience. During summer, picnicking in the herb garden can't be beat. Ron makes one-of-a-kind wine; Susan creates food, labels, and experiences; her mother Paula is the "artist-in-residence." Daughter Amelia has already drawn her first label, and son Alex counts the days till he can drive daddy's forklift. Vive la famille!

Top: Ron and Susan Bunnell toast the new vintage.
Photograph by Andréa Johnson

Middle: Fraîche, the newest white Rhône blend from the Bunnell Family.
Photograph by Andréa Johnson

Bottom: Heirloom tomatoes and fresh herbs from the garden, red wine from Wine o'Clock, and pizza from the wood-burning oven.
Photograph by Andréa Johnson

Facing page: The Bunnell Family wine bar, Wine o'Clock, nestled in an extensive herb and vegetable garden. Lavender, thyme, chives, eggplant…a salad just waiting to be picked!
Photograph by Shannen Anderson

Buty Winery

Walla Walla

The artistic creations at Buty Winery—pronounced "beauty"—have dazzled connoisseurs since the winery was founded in 2000. They have also earned across-the-board raves from the wine press and a bevy of Top 100 honors. As a result, Buty's visionary wines have come to be recognized as benchmarks for quality, creativity, and value, offering a rare intersection of the three that stunningly portrays the essence of Washington State. As Paul Gregutt, one of Washington's leading critics, said, "Buty wines, both white and red, consistently show the sort of nuance and depth that mark the world's best."

Caleb Foster and Nina Buty established their artisan, family-run winery to showcase exquisite Washington State blends. With more than two decades of professional winemaking experience spread across three continents with such renowned wineries as Woodward Canyon, Matua, Chateau Ste. Michelle, and others, Caleb has established a reputation for his mastery of the blend.

Guided by the philosophy that growth occurs from body to mind to soul to spirit—with each level building on the last to create a more complex whole—Caleb, Nina, and consulting winemaker Zelma Long embrace a cumulative, artistic process that results in great wine. This creative approach led Caleb and Nina to produce their pioneering Rediviva® cabernet–syrah blends. These wines were the first of their kind in Washington State and continue to set the standard.

Top: Buty's traditional dry Bordeaux white blend on a morning bed of handpicked sémillon grapes.
Photograph by Caleb Foster

Bottom: Nina Buty and Caleb Foster in their Rockgarden Estate in Walla Walla Valley.
Photograph by Tom Olander

Facing page: Rockgarden Estate vintage 2011 grenache certified organic by Oregon Tilth.
Photograph by Caleb Foster

In the vineyard, Caleb personally directs viticulture from winter through autumn, guiding pruning, shoot positioning, pre-véraison cluster thinning, and hand harvesting. Relationships developed professionally over 20 years with renowned properties offer Buty the finest of the state's fruit, with estate-grown vineyards providing the majority of Buty's production. These estate vineyards include Buty's organically farmed Rockgarden Estate Vineyard, its prized nine-acre block in Phinny Hill Vineyard, and a section of Conner Lee Vineyard. Located in the famous Milton cobblestones section of Walla Walla Valley, Rockgarden—which is densely planted to top clones of syrah and cabernet sauvignon, as well as other varieties—was designed by Buty with one wine in mind: the Rediviva of the Stones.

Within the cellar, Caleb applies a light hand, ensuring that each of Buty's blends continues to metamorphose into its own distinctive personality that is rooted in the soil of its site. Embracing techniques that have catapulted him to the forefront of several winemaking movements—such as a commitment to using little or no new oak, a belief that early picking retains purity, aromatics, and acidity, and a dedication to natural winemaking

without the use of additions or enhancements—every winemaking step makes evident Caleb's soulful approach.

And then there is the BEAST. The alter ego of Buty, BEAST is a label of limited, often single-vineyard wines that are crafted with absolutely no rules. With BEAST, new varietals, new vineyards, and even strange new wines can dictate the offering—Caleb and Nina base these creations on whatever inspires them each year. Unified by the people who produce them, both Buty and BEAST present extraordinary texture, structured backbone, a focus on lovely fruit, and a balance of approachability and ability to age—elements every wine lover will appreciate.

Above left: Caleb unearthing buried canes protected from winter cold, which yielded Rockgarden's 2011 harvest.
Photograph courtesy of Buty Winery

Top: Hand-harvesting and field-sorting of Rockgarden Estate's first vintage in October 2010.
Photograph by Nina Buty

Bottom: Handpicked 2010 vintage Rockgarden mourvèdre on a fine dry October harvest day in Walla Walla Valley.
Photograph by Nina Buty

Facing page: Buty's first mourvèdre from Rockgarden Estate getting the love and attention it deserves before being foot-stomped to ferment.
Photograph by Nina Buty

WINE & FARE

Buty Conner Lee Vineyard Chardonnay, Columbia Valley
Delicious with Washington State Dungeness crab.

Buty Sémillon, Sauvignon & Muscadelle, Columbia Valley
Lovely with mushroom ravioli.

Buty Rediviva of the Stones, Walla Walla Valley
Exquisite with spring lamb.

Buty Columbia Rediviva, Phinny Hill Vineyard Estate Grown,
Horse Heavan Hills
Wonderful with pepper steak.

Tastings
Open to the public Monday through Saturday

Canoe Ridge Vineyard
Walla Walla

In 1805, historical figures Meriwether Lewis and William Clark explored the Columbia River and made a number of scientific and geological discoveries. Among these was an unusually shaped ridge that resembled an overturned canoe. Aptly declared Canoe Ridge by the adventurers, the ridge and adjacent vicinity—largely inhabited by wildlife and acres upon acres of vines—have preserved the name for over two centuries. Founded in 1994, Canoe Ridge Vineyard is a prosperous source of choice Bordeaux-style grapes within the Horse Heaven Hills appellation. The vineyard is a leading resource of estate-grown merlot, cabernet sauvignon, and chardonnay varietals.

Upon harvest, the grapes travel from the vineyard to the winery, located in Walla Walla. A renovated engine house acts as the estate tasting room as well as a cellar for barrels of small test lots and reserve bottles. Next door, most of the production takes place in a newly constructed, energy-conscious facility. Under the direction of head winemaker Bill Murray—not the comedian/actor—vintages celebrated by salient publications such as *Wine Enthusiast* and *Wine Spectator* magazines are crafted and bottled in hopes of earning more 90-plus ratings next year.

Top: Winemaker Bill Murray.

Bottom: Wine tasting in the barrel room.

Facing page: Merlot vines on the estate vineyard.
Photographs by Andréa Johnson

Cascade Cliffs
Vineyard & Winery

Wishram

Every winery feels that it's unique. Whether it's the winery's history, where it's located, or what it produces, setting itself apart from other wineries is imperative. Cascade Cliffs Vineyard & Winery has several attributes that make it a gem among Washington's artisan wineries. The estate vineyard is home to some of the Pacific Northwest's original plantings of Piedmont varietals—wine grapes originally from its namesake region in northwest Italy. Barbera, dolcetto, and nebbiolo thrive here, and the winery's numerous awards have helped establish Cascade Cliffs as a well-respected Columbia Valley vineyard.

Located alongside the Columbia River and in the rain shadow of the Cascade mountain range, the vineyard benefits from long, warm growing seasons. Intense light reflection from the river and heat from the nearby basalt cliffs create an environment that is ideal for the unique varietals that thrive here. The vineyard also lays claim to the rare symphony varietal, a cross of muscat of Alexandria and grenache gris. This is the only white wine that Cascade Cliffs produces, and they are one of the only symphony producers in the Northwest.

Owner and winemaker Robert Lorkowski founded Cascade Cliffs in 1997 with just five acres to his name, later purchasing the property and adding acre after acre of additional vines to include some of his now-signature varietals. Cascade Cliffs is known to produce the most intense and concentrated examples of barbera. Packed with dark, rich cherry and berry flavors and an intense, lingering finish, this wine is one of the more sought-after bottles in the Northwest. And fans of Italy's prestigious Barolo and Barbaresco wines—made from the nebbiolo grape—appreciate the elegance and complexity of the winery's estate nebbiolo. Additionally, Cascade Cliffs vineyard also grows and produces syrah, cabernet sauvignon, merlot, and zinfandel.

Top: The entrance sign hints at the massive timbers, stone, and iron that are used throughout the winery and its grounds.
Photograph by Andréa Johnson

Bottom: Visitors are welcomed into the front entrance of the winery's rustic tasting room by festive lights.
Photograph by Jared Germain

Facing page: A birds-eye view of the estate vineyard, looking south with the Columbia River and rolling hills of nearby Oregon in the background.
Photograph by Andréa Johnson

The winery's interior and exterior are clad with massive pine timbers as well as cedar and black walnut for a distinct, yet cozy, Northwestern feel. Guests feel right at home in either of the vineyard's two tasting rooms as they savor unique sips in an authentic environment.

Many of the wines are made from Cascade Cliff's own estate fruit, and the winery features red wines that are never filtered or fined. In addition, Robert has infused biodynamic techniques into his vineyard practice to achieve the grape's maximum potential. Attention is paid to lunar cycles with specific, ideal days designated for picking the fruit and pruning the vines. It's all part of the natural, rustic ambience that sets Cascade Cliffs Winery & Vineyards apart.

Above: The vineyard and winery are surrounded by the area's natural beauty, which encourages skiing, windsurfing, and rock climbing. Looking west, visitors can view majestic Mt. Hood, the Columbia River, and Horsethief Butte.
Photograph by Jared Germain

Left: A family affair. Annya, Robert, and John Lorkowski take part in punching down the year's harvested grapes.
Photograph by Andréa Johnson

Facing page: Winter settles onto the estate vineyard. Snow-capped basalt cliffs to the north overlook the vines, creating a winter wonderland.
Photograph by Jared Germain

WINE & FARE

Estate Barbera
Exceptional with grilled meats.

Estate Nebbiolo
Pairs well with wild mushrooms.

Estate Symphony
Delicious with spicy Asian cuisine.

Columbia Valley Zinfandel
Brilliant with flourless, dark chocolate torte.

Tastings
Open to the public daily, year-round
Also available at Hood River tasting room, Oregon

Cave B Estate Winery

Quincy

A place of learning and natural beauty situated in the heart of Washington wine country—that's Cave B Estate Winery. Vincent and Carol Bryan acquired the Columbia Valley land after searching the state for topography similar to that of the great wine regions of France. Their fruitful venture has helped put Washington on the map, bringing with it the creation of wines greater than they could have dreamed.

In 1980, when the Bryans first planted the vineyard, that part of the state did not grow any vinifera grapes. The land in the area had been used for cattle grazing and growing alfalfa, wheat, and corn, but the variety in both soil and microclimate, as well as its jaw-dropping site amid gorges and valleys, called for a noble purpose. Shortly after planting grapes, Champs de Brionne Winery was born, but the remote location made attracting tasters a challenge. Once the Bryans discovered the perfect acoustics of a natural amphitheater formed by a little bowl carved into the gorge, music and wine became intertwined. The summer music theater quickly gained popularity until, over time, what is now known as The Gorge Amphitheatre attracted 20,000 guests per concert. Attendees sipped wine while enjoying the performances, and knowledge of the vineyard's wines spread. Listeners went away awed by the innate power of the landscape, and the Bryans knew they had found a sublimely special place.

Top: Cave B Estate Winery produces a total of 5,000 cases of premium red, white, and rosé wines per year.
Photograph by Jeremy Quant

Bottom: The 110 acres of estate vineyards produce 17 varieties, an unusually large number. From merlot to tempranillo, chardonnay to sangiovese, the diversity is a result of the area's unique geography and microclimates.
Photograph by Cave B Estate Winery

Facing page: The estate vineyards surround Cave B Inn & Spa, where wine lovers go to linger in the stunning landscape.
Photograph by Yanmei Shi

Realizing the vineyards needed to be worthy of such amazing earth, the Bryans took a hiatus from winemaking in order to focus on developing mature vines and grapes. By 2000, the time had come to open a winery again, this time a smaller boutique one: Cave B Estate Winery. Cave B makes estate wines from the 17 varietals carefully tended to across the magnificent vineyards. Winemaker Alfredo "Freddy" Arredondo's goal is to consistently produce superior quality wines, regardless of varietal, that express terroir through the best of the grapes. He crafts wines that have garnered attention across Washington and further abroad, including red blends of Bordeaux French varietals cabernet sauvignon, malbec, merlot, and cabernet franc, as well as tempranillo, chardonnay, and riesling. Of the production yield, 90 percent is sold on-site to encourage consumers to experience the wine's full essence through seeing, tasting, smelling, and touching the land where it was grown and made.

From the beauty of the site to the diversity of soil and microclimate in the vineyards to the top-notch, dedicated team, food-friendly wines, and eco-friendly, unobtrusive architecture, Cave B Estate Winery encompasses something truly wonderful: a little slice of heaven on earth.

Top: Cave B's head winemaker since 2007, Freddy Arredondo brings his joint culinary-winemaking background to the creation of Cave B's wonderfully food-friendly wines.
Photograph by Bruce E. Hutson

Middle: The combination of rolling estate vineyards coupled with dramatic Columbia River Gorge views makes for an exquisite wine tasting experience.
Photograph by Jeremy Quant

Bottom: The Cave B tasting room pops with energy during concert weekends at the neighboring Gorge Amphitheatre.
Photograph by Yanmei Shi

Facing page: Some of the oldest vineyards in Washington State, Cave B's hold a special place in the state's winemaking history.
Photograph by Sam Heim

WINE & FARE

Riesling
Pair with pad thai or almost any Thai dish.

Cuvée du Soleil
Perfect with braised beef or hearty grilled steak.

Malbec
Goes beautifully with game such as elk or venison, but also great with a nice peppercorn-crusted steak.

Chardonnay
Tremendous with classically prepared roasted chicken and a sunchoke purée.

Tastings
Times vary by season, please check website for details

Watch a video of winemaker Alfredo "Freddy" Arredondo discussing the unique terroir of the vineyards and the crisp, fresh flavors of the wines.

CAVE B
Estate Winery

Chandler Reach Vineyards
Benton City

While it's true that one never really knows where inspiration may strike, the picturesque landscape of Tuscany is certainly ripe with possibility. And it was while on vacation in the beautiful storied Italian backdrop that Len Parris gained the insight and, yes, the inspiration to bring a bit of the Old World back to his Washington zip code.

As a natural-born entrepreneur would while surveying the Tuscan vineyards, Len mentioned that he could "do" this in Washington. "Do" soon evolved into Chandler Reach Vineyards. But not without nudging from friends, an amazing partnership in wife Jane, a winemaking education, exhaustive planning, and trusted alliances with the best professionals—for Len does not let a single detail evade notice.

Though the Chandler Reach Vineyards' tagline says "Believe Your Eyes," you may have to blink twice. The family-owned vineyard is located in Yakima Valley's Benton City, perfectly positioned on a north-facing slope overlooking Red Mountain. Surveying the 42 acres of estate vineyards, one is transported to an awing Tuscan villa surrounded by gorgeous lands, abundant with high-quality fruit. And that's the point; Len and his wife literally want their guests to feel "20 minutes from Tuscany."

Top: Looking out toward the back lawn with Red Mountain on the horizon.

Bottom: Sangiovese clusters love long summer days laden with warmth and cool nights for ripening.

Facing page: The north-facing slope boasts a view of Red Mountain.
Photographs by Andréa Johnson

Chandler Reach maintains a low crop load to insure superior quality and intense flavors. From its very first foray into wine production with a blend called Monte Regalo in 2001—which just happened to nab a gold medal and Best of Class—the vineyards' ever-evolving wines continue to earn medals and high scores. Blessed with excellent terroir in an area considered to be among the warmest in the state, Chandler Reach grows only red varietals including cabernet sauvignon, cabernet franc, merlot, syrah, and sangiovese. Carefully managed viticultural practices ensure premium grapes.

Maintaining a temperature of 58 degrees in the underground barrel storage room also contributes to the wines' quality. The winemaker allows the wines to take their shape without over-manipulation. Generally racked four to five times with gentle pumping and gravity feeding when possible, the red wines are left to age gracefully in French oak for 22 to 24 months.

Chandler Reach wines truly are representative of the terroir. Given the fact that Len and Jane have the option to pick at the perfect time and ripeness, the fruit is in balance. This advantage provides Chandler Reach wines with a certain depth, structure, and finish, resulting in the elegant yet powerful aspects of most of its wines.

Len and Jane invite visitors to their bit of Tuscany; whether they fall under the spell of their wines, the breathtaking geography, or the event-filled villa, above all else, the couple just wants guests to be inspired.

Top: Owners Len and Jane Parris enjoying a glass of wine inside their Tuscan-style tasting room.

Bottom: A sampling of Chandler Reach and Parris Estate Reserve wine labels.

Facing page: The breathtaking Tuscan-inspired villa offers banquet space in addition to the tasting room.
Photographs by Andréa Johnson

Corella
Excellent with roast beef or spicy chicken cacciatore.

Cabernet Franc
Delightful with lasagna, Middle Eastern fare, or Greek cuisine.

Monte Regalo
Superb with poultry, red meat, pork, pastas, and salads.

Tastings
Seasonal and by appointment

Chandler Reach
V I N E Y A R D S

Chateau Ste. Michelle
Woodinville

Every wine drinker in Washington knows Chateau Ste. Michelle. Not only is it the oldest winery—the first founded in the state—it produces some of the best wine available, including first-rate riesling, cabernet, chardonnay, and merlot. A rich history dating back to the repeal of Prohibition combined with world-class vineyards and talented winemakers have made Chateau Ste. Michelle a favorite brand as well as a popular tourist destination.

After Prohibition, the Pommerelle Wine Company and the National Wine Company were founded; in 1954 they merged into American Wine Growers. 1967 saw the creation of the firm's Ste. Michelle Vintners label with legendary California winemaker and consultant André Tchelistcheff at the helm. Riesling has long been a specialty: Ste. Michelle was among the first to plant the grape in Washington, and in 1974 won the Los Angeles Times' riesling blind tasting with its 1972 Johannisberg riesling. National acclaim followed, and in 1976 the line of wines received its own French-style château in Woodinville and a name change to match—Chateau Ste. Michelle. Built on the 105-acre estate established in 1912 by lumber baron Frederick Stimson, Chateau Ste. Michelle quickly became one of the top tourist attractions in the Seattle area.

Today Chateau Ste. Michelle wines are made by head winemaker Bob Bertheau. The gifted vintner melds Old World tradition with New World innovation and focuses on a portfolio of chardonnay, sauvignon blanc, pinot gris, merlot, cabernet sauvignon, syrah, and of course riesling. The winery sources from its 3,500 dry and sunny acres in the Columbia Valley—including Cold Creek Vineyard, its 811-acre eastern Washington debut vineyard planted in 1973—as well as its vineyard at Canoe Ridge Estate planted in 1991. White wines are made

Top: Chateau Ste. Michelle head winemaker Bob Bertheau joined the winery in 2003 after 16 years of winemaking in Sonoma County, California.

Bottom: Chateau Ste. Michelle offers winery tours and tastings daily with an array of tasting experiences.

Facing page: Guests can enjoy a picnic on the winery's expansive 105-acre estate, once home to Seattle lumber baron Frederick Stimson in the early 1900s.
Photographs by Andréa Johnson

at the Woodinville château; red wines at the Canoe Ridge Estate satellite winery and 559-acre vineyard. This allows Bob to build programs tailored to the specific needs and features of each, whether he wants to draw out a varietal characteristic or a terroir flavor.

The winery's scenic grounds make it perfect for picnics, and in summer a popular outdoor concert series takes over. Guided tours and tastings happen daily—visitors can choose from a variety of tastings—and there are monthly chef dinners, wine and cheese nights, and other special events.

Chateau Ste. Michelle considers itself a champion of riesling, encouraging other wineries in North America to follow suit. Befitting a riesling authority, it has eight different rieslings to showcase the versatility of the varietal and the regional styles within the Columbia Valley—the foremost American

region producing riesling. The riesling lineup includes Eroica Riesling, a partnership with Chateau Ste. Michelle and Ernst Loosen of Germany, which has become the benchmark for American luxury riesling. In addition to that, it's also a leader in sustainability and viticultural research. After all, Cold Creek and Canoe Ridge Estate vineyards earned third-party sustainable certification for LIVE and Salmon-Safe in 2009. No matter in what arena, the winery is a true pioneer not just in the state but in all of North America. It regularly inspires other wineries to greatness and to the awareness of possibilities, while supplying wine lovers across the nation with great-tasting wine.

Above left: Planted in 1991, Chateau Ste. Michelle's vineyard at Canoe Ridge Estate is located in eastern Washington in the Horse Heaven Hills AVA.

Above right: Guests experience the ultimate in wine tasting with an expert wine specialist in the winery's library.

Facing page: Chateau Ste. Michelle is one of the top visitor attractions in the Seattle area and home to a popular outdoor summer concert series.
Photographs by Andréa Johnson

Horse Heaven Vineyard Sauvignon Blanc
Pair with seared scallops and asparagus.

Dry Riesling
Serve with grilled prawns with Indian chutney.

Cold Creek Vineyard Cabernet Sauvignon
Pair with a grilled flatiron steak.

Ethos Late Harvest Riesling
Great with riesling-poached pears.

Tastings
Open to the public daily, year-round
Also available at Chateau Ste. Michelle's Canoe Ridge Estate
Tasting Gallery, seasonally

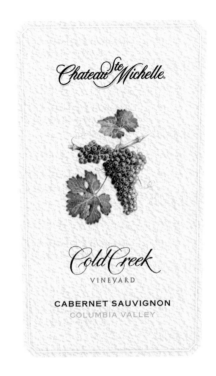

Chinook Wines

Prosser

A set of sun-soaked vineyards lies nestled in Washington's Yakima Valley—one of the state's first-established American Viticultural Areas. It was here in 1983 that Clay Mackey and Kay Simon began harvesting the grapes for their winery, Chinook Wines. The establishment's charming, rustic vibe capitalizes on an old cherry farm's original buildings, renovated to serve as modern-day facilities—like the 1928 farmhouse as the tasting room. Guests can sample wines from Kay's grandmother's old buffet, while relishing a slice of the winemaker's homemade bread.

Clay and Kay both studied winemaking and viticulture at the University of California at Davis, and met at Chateau Ste. Michelle. In 1983, with borrowed equipment and much determination, the talented couple established Chinook Wines—named after the warm coastal winds of the Pacific Northwest. Within a year, they debuted their first wine, a 1983 sauvignon blanc, and tied the knot two days later.

Every drop of Chinook Wines is bottled in-house with high-tech Italian equipment—a rarity for a winery of its size. Chinook produces blended vineyard site wines such as sémillon, sauvignon blanc, chardonnay, merlot, cabernet sauvignon, and the Chinook Yakima Valley cabernet franc. The latter is crafted in both a red wine and a dry rosé and is a highlight for Chinook, which also produces a blend dubbed Yakima Valley Red Wine and White Wine. Guests frequently enjoy picnics on the shaded lawn at Chinook Wines in between tours and tastings—all the while feeling quite at home, just the way Clay and Kay intended.

Top: Chinook's estate vineyard surrounds the winery and supplies it with high-quality grapes for its signature cabernet franc wines.
Photograph by Jennifer Kennard

Middle: Kay Simon and Clay Mackey, assisted by family and friends, have put the 1928-era buildings to new use as a working winery, tasting room, and warehouse space. The surrounding garden is a favorite picnic spot in the warmer months.
Photograph by Chinook Wines

Bottom: The winery's rustic tasting room is augmented by state-of-the-art winery equipment, which lets winemaker Kay and viticulturist Clay make their well-regarded wines.
Photograph by Laurie Black, Laurie Black Photography

Facing page: Winemakers Kay and Clay and restaurateurs Tom Douglas and Jackie Cross meet at Prosser Farm to blend a special wine for the 20th anniversary of Tom and Jackie's restaurant, Dahlia Lounge.
Photograph by Washington Tasting Room Magazine

Col Solare Winery
Benton City

The experience and vision that has made Col Solare Winery into what it is today can be traced back more than 600 years. That's how long co-owner Marchese Piero Antinori's family has been involved in winemaking in Tuscany. Within Washington, the winery's roots are found in Chateau Ste. Michelle, a legend in and of itself.

Marchese Piero, whose Solaia and Tignanello wines revolutionized the Italian wine industry in the 1970s, ventured to Washington in the early '90s and found not only an emerging wine region with innovative, amazing vinifera but also Old World character reminiscent of his home. At Chateau St. Michelle—the Northwest's oldest and most acclaimed winery—Marchese Piero saw mutual philosophies regarding grape growing and winemaking and knew that this was an opportunity not to be missed.

With that kind of Italian-Washington pedigree, the success of Col Solare was a foregone conclusion. After spending several years determining the best location for a singularly focused winery, Ted Baseler—Chateau Ste. Michelle's president and CEO—and Marchese Piero discovered a site on Red Mountain where the winery and estate vineyard reflected the two partners' aesthetics and traditions that combine Old World and New World.

Italian for "shining hill," Col Solare was established with cabernet sauvignon as the dominant varietal. The partners carefully blend the two distinct grape-growing and winemaking cultures into a powerful yet silky style, focusing on the Antinori family's philosophy: the endless pursuit of quality.

Top: Col Solare produces Washington's top cabernet sauvignon-based red wine.
Photograph by Andrëa Johnson

Bottom: An important part of the process occurs in the barricaia at Col Solare's estate winery on Red Mountain.
Photograph courtesy of Col Solare Estate Winery and Vineyard

Facing page: The vineyard is a beautiful sight at Col Solare Estate Winery and Vineyard.
Photograph by Kevin Cruff

The estate vineyard was planted according to Marchese Piero's specifications for his vineyards in Tuscany and Umbria, matching the orientation, spacing, and density to the site to ensure uniform ripening and fruit quality. Planted in a radial pattern to fit the site's natural contours and with the winery at its apex, the vines follow a single-cordon training system to further encourage uniformity.

The winery overlooks the fan-shaped vineyard and has stunning views of Mount Adams and the Horse Heaven Hills. The links to old and new are immediately evident. A traditional barrel chai, featuring three rooms where the wine is handled by gravity, sits next to the modern cellar, which leads to a 56-foot-high bell tower reminiscent of the Old World—still rung on special occasions—and into a contemporary reception area. Visitors to the west side of the state can enjoy Col Solare wines and experience a taste of Red Mountain at the Col Solare Bottega, located within Chateau Ste. Michelle in Woodinville.

This destined partnership results in award-winning wines full of fruit that are rich but balanced on the palate. The signature cabernet sauvignon-based red wine is preceded by Shining Hill, a declassified red blend released a vintage ahead of the flagship wine.

Top: Wine and cheese pairings are a popular activity for visitors to the Red Mountain winery.
Photograph by Andréa Johnson

Middle: Col Solare winemaker Marcus Notaro (second from left) and his team craft each vintage of Col Solare in the winery's state-of-the-art cellar, built in 2006.
Photograph by Andréa Johnson

Bottom: Visitors to the winery's Red Mountain tasting room enjoy two vintages of Col Solare and private tours by appointment.
Photograph by Andréa Johnson

Facing page: Cabernet sauvignon grapes grow exceptionally well at the winery's Red Mountain vineyard, planted in 2007.
Photograph by Andréa Johnson

WINE & FARE

Col Solare
Amazing with a braised short ribs with roasted root vegetables.

Shining Hill
Exceptional with antipasto, robust cheeses, and a wood-fired pizza.

Tastings
Available at Col Solare and Col Solare Bottega
Open by appointment daily

Columbia Crest

Paterson

Overlooking the Columbia River, boasting a breathtaking view of Washington, a manor fit for the French countryside proves to be even more than what the eye beholds. The enchanted setting of Columbia Crest conceals an underground winemaking operation that maintains year-round temperatures and humidity control for barrels of award-winning vintages. Just above, fruits flourish during the hot days and cool nights on acres upon acres of vineyards that are part of Horse Heaven Hills, one of the newest and most unique AVAs in Washington State.

Fed by water pulled from the conveniently located Columbia River, grapes in this region are cared for using drip irrigation, which mitigates the effects of harsh environmental conditions. Fruit planted on south-facing slopes benefit from strong winds blown in through the Columbia Gorge, cooling the grapes and damage to the vines.

From its establishment in 1983 to present day, Columbia Crest has commissioned only three winemakers. Becoming the third winemaker within Columbia Crest's thriving history is an intimidating position for anyone to accept, but Juan Muñoz Oca is not just anyone. A third-generation winemaker and lifelong student of viticulture, Juan was digging in the dirt while other little boys in Mendoza, Argentina, were playing ball and chasing girls. His passion for grapes grew early, planted and nurtured by his cellar master grandfather; Juan naturally adopted the love of winemaking synonymous with his family values and Spanish heritage.

Top: Cabernet sauvignon grapes from the Columbia Crest Estate Vineyard will go into the winery's highly acclaimed Reserve Cabernet Sauvignon.
Photograph by Andréa Johnson

Bottom: Columbia Crest's estate vineyard is located in the Horse Heaven Hills appellation of south central Washington along the Columbia River.
Photograph by Kevin Cruff

Facing page: Columbia Crest winery, founded in 1983, is located in Paterson, adjacent to the Columbia River in eastern Washington.
Photograph by Andréa Johnson

After polishing his skills in the Bordeaux region of France, Australia, Argentina, and Spain, Juan began interning with the viticulture team at Ste. Michelle Wine Estates and in 2003 joined Columbia Crest. Earning degrees from Argentina's National University of Cuyo in agricultural engineering as well as winemaking, Juan blends traditional techniques with new technology and personal creativity to produce world-class wines.

Columbia Crest is the proud producer of four tiers of wines, each of which is tailored to a unique demographic of wine aficionados. Its tiers Reserve, Grand Estates, H3, and Two Vines have garnered international attention. With more than 16 wines on *Wine Spectator*'s Top 100 list since 2010, and as the only Washington winery to earn *Wine Spectator*'s wine of the year in 2009, Columbia Crest continues to demonstrate leadership in crafting wines that are acclaimed by critics and consumers alike.

Top: A group of winery guests enjoy a tasting in the Petit Chai with winemaker Juan Muñoz Oca.
Photograph by Andréa Johnson

Middle: The Walter Clore Private Reserve Red Wine is dedicated to Dr. Walter Clore, Washington's pioneering viticultural researcher who shaped the state's wine industry.
Photograph by Columbia Crest winery

Bottom: Guests enjoy wine by the lobby fireplace, which was built in 1983. The mantel was sourced from a redwood tank used by Washington's winemaking pioneers to store fortified wines.
Photograph by Andréa Johnson

Facing page: Winemaker Juan Muñoz Oca in the Petit Chai—a winery-within-a-winery—where the top-tier reserve wines are meticulously handcrafted.
Photograph by Andréa Johnson

WINE & FARE

H3 Merlot
Pair with cedar plank salmon with merlot reduction and wild mushrooms.

Grand Estates Chardonnay
Pair with Dungeness crab cakes and balsamic-tossed green spring mix.

Reserve Cabernet Sauvignon
Pair with roasted pork tenderloin with fig cabernet sauce.

Tastings
Open to the public daily, year-round

COLUMBIA·CREST®

Columbia Winery
Woodinville

L ike many wineries in the northwest, Columbia Winery began in the humble setting of an ambitious professional's garage. Unlike any other winery, it became Washington's first premium winery, founded in 1962 by ten friends, six of whom were University of Washington professors. Originally known as Associated Vintners, the group believed that classic European vinifera vines would thrive in Washington's climate and that fine wine could be made from its mineral-led soil and natural aptitude for grapes. Honored in the book *Vintage* by Hugh Johnson for their industry-defining actions, the friends began their wine revolution in the garage of Dr. Lloyd Woodburne—the winery's first winemaker—with grapes grown in the Columbia and Yakima Valley appellations, where long sunny days and cool clear nights were intensified by the surrounding Cascade Mountains.

Winemaker David Lake, titled "dean of Washington winemakers" by *Wine Spectator* and *Decanter* magazine, joined Columbia Winery in 1979, bringing with him the synergy of art and science and the continued spirit of innovation. By introducing new varietals to the state, such as syrah, cabernet franc, and pinot gris, David became renowned for his experimentation and for producing the first series of vineyard-designate wines in Washington. He retired from Columbia Winery in 2006, but lives on in the rich history that he helped create.

Following in his footsteps, current winemaker Kerry Norton enjoys experimenting with varietals and blends in the estate's Small Lot Series, as well as perfecting bottles of riesling, cabernet sauvignon, merlot, chardonnay, syrah, gewürztraminer, pinot gris, and cabernet franc for the estate's remaining three series. When he is not perusing the vineyards to check vines, he is searching for rare stones like granite, schist, gneiss, marble, and quartzite, as well

Top: Viognier vines are beautiful in the fall.

Bottom: The first plantings of syrah in the state of Washington were planted at Red Willow Vineyard in Yakima Valley, with the first bottling done by Columbia Winery.

Facing page: Fall colors encompass the South Chapel block at Red Willow Vineyard in Yakima Valley, where some of Columbia Winery's best cabernet sauvignon and syrah are sourced.
Photographs by Andréa Johnson

as indigenous rocks to the region including basalt, petrified wood, opal, agate, and serpentine. The estate's Stone Cutter series is named in honor of the winemaker's favored pastime of polishing forgotten rocks.

Located in the scenic Woodinville wine country, Columbia Winery is a landmark Victorian mansion surrounded by English gardens. Here guests can enjoy exclusive Small Lot cabernet franc, unoaked chardonnay, sangiovese, barbera, malbec, and viognier—produced for wine club members and tasting room sojourners only—or other releases from the Stone Cutter, Core, and Vineyard Designate series. Event catering from some of the best chefs in the greater Seattle area helps enhance the total sensorial experience with divine pairings and impeccable service. Exquisite amenities, such as an extensive outdoor terrace, can be enjoyed fully during summertime private parties and regal receptions.

Above: Columbia Winery winemaker Kerry Norton (left) and Red Willow Vineyard owner Mike Sauer (right) overlook the Yakima Valley.

Left: The small stone chapel at the Red Willow Vineyard adds to the Old World charm of the property.

Facing page: Visitors to the winery's tasting room and hospitality center in Woodinville can sample a portfolio of award-winning Washington State wines.
Photographs by Andréa Johnson

Cellarmaster's Riesling
Pair with spicy Asian cuisine or desserts such as rhubarb-apple crisp, crème brûlée, or peach cobbler.

Small Lot Riesling
Pair with spicy pad thai or lemon chicken.

Cabernet Sauvignon
Pair with French cassoulet slow-cooked with white beans, duck confit, sausage, and pork.

Syrah
Pair with grilled lamb or pork tenderloin with cherry compote.

Tastings
Open to the public daily, year-round

Watch a video of winemaker Kerry Norton discussing Red Willow Vineyard and introducing the crew involved with Columbia Winery.

EST. 1962

COLUMBIA WINERY

CELEBRATING

50 YEARS

WASHINGTON'S FIRST
PREMIUM WINERY

Corliss Estates Winery

Walla Walla

Corliss Estates Winery's guiding principle is embodied in Ralph Waldo Emerson's quote, "Adopt the pace of nature, her secret is patience." Nothing at Corliss is rushed. In 1999, Michael and Lauri Corliss purchased the dilapidated Red and White Brand bakery building in Walla Walla and embarked on a nine-year restoration of the historic structure. Now home to Corliss, the building is one of the most visually stunning, state-of-the-art winemaking facilities in America.

While renovating the facility, the Corlisses began assembling their vineyard portfolio, strategically acquiring three vineyards: Blue Mountain Estate in the Walla Walla AVA, Red Mountain Vineyard in the Red Mountain AVA, and Blackrock Vineyard in the Columbia Valley AVA. They also planted a fourth vineyard, the meticulously planned Red Mountain Canyons Vineyard, in the Red Mountain AVA. All vineyards are farmed to exacting standards, utilizing sustainable viticulture methods. A small portion of the best grapes are crafted into Corliss wines, while the remaining fruit is reserved for other top Washington wineries.

Michael and Lauri's winemaking philosophy is built around natural, gentle processes, as they make decisions based on taste rather than a predetermined formula. The fruit is hand-picked and sorted in the vineyard, and then hand-sorted again at the winery before being gravity-fed into custom French oak fermenters that maximize the extraction and integration of tannins. Native yeast strains develop through slow, cool fermentations, further enhancing precise flavors and aromatic elements for velvety texture and complexity, the hallmarks of Corliss wines.

Top: Sunrise in the vineyard.

Bottom: Corliss bottles aging in the cellar.

Facing page: Blue Mountain Estate Vineyard.
Photographs by Colby Kuschatka

Likewise, every barrel is meticulously followed through each stage, and only the best lots are selected for the final blend. To ensure seamless integration and the development of secondary aromas, Corliss wines are matured two additional years in the bottle before being released. The results are apparent: substantial yet refined, exhibiting beautiful delineation of flavor, aroma, and texture. Critics have been astounded that the wines are sufficiently structured to age for decades, yet are remarkably developed, supple, and ready to drink when released.

At the beginning of their journey, Lauri noted that "the learning curve was steep." Yet with patience and precision, the inaugural 2003 vintage of their Red Wine was named Washington's most outstanding wine. In 2008, Corliss was named the best new winery by *Seattle* magazine.

The winery produces three wines: a cabernet sauvignon, a Bordeaux-style blend called Red Wine, and a syrah. Though Corliss is not open to the public, the family holds private spring and fall release events for registry members to pick up their annual allotment and sample future vintages.

Time and a reverence for Old World techniques set Corliss wines apart. With a goal to produce Washington wines that are a contribution to the *grands vins* of the world, Michael and Lauri Corliss take no shortcuts in achieving this vision.

Top: Blue Mountain Estate Vineyard.
Photograph by Andréa Johnson

Middle: Lauri and Michael Corliss in the Corliss production facility.
Photograph by Colby Kuschatka

Bottom: A sampling of Corliss wines
Photograph by Colby Kuschatka

Facing page: Corliss Estates Winery.
Photograph by Colby Kuschatka

WINE & FARE

Corliss Cabernet Sauvignon
Exquisite with lamb shoulder, braised Belgian endive,
and a blue cheese gratin dauphinois.

Corliss Red Wine
Delicious with duck confit-stuffed quail with orzo risotto
and Périgueux sauce.

Corliss Syrah
Delectable with roast rack of venison, fresh green peppercorns,
and chestnut confit.

Tastings
By invitation only

Watch a video of Michael and Lauri Corliss discussing
why Washington is an ideal location for making wine.

CORLISS®

Cougar Crest
Estate Winery

Walla Walla

C ougar Crest Estate Winery evolved from a love of agriculture, a fascination with grape growing, and a focus on the intertwined disciplines of science and art that is winemaking. Founders David and Deborah Hansen, husband and wife who were each born and raised in Washington State, grew up with an impressive agricultural work ethic. While David became an electrician and then a veterinarian, and Deborah a pharmacist, they dreamed of owning and keeping their own land as farmers. The couple moved to California, where they explored the area's many winemaking regions and learned about terroir before the phrase "wine tourism" was even coined. Though they loved California, the couple longed to return home.

In 1996, with two children and three cats, they settled in the Walla Walla Valley, home to David's extended family. There they developed apple, cherry, and plum orchards, and a year later seized the opportunity to become part of the local wine community by laying out their first 10-acre vineyard. Each year saw more success, and in 2001 David and Deborah registered the winery and became vigneron and winemaker, respectively.

The winery originally placed emphasis on Bordeaux wines, but the allure of syrah could not be denied. A little-known but up-and-coming white grape called viognier was also planted. Over the years, these have become the mainstays of the Cougar Crest wines, with malbec, petit verdot, tempranillo, and grenache added for blending and to increase variety. Exquisite attention to detail has brought national and international attention. Each passing year, the list of honors—gold and double gold awards, Best of Class awards, and consistent ratings above 90 points—continues to grow.

Top: Founders Dave and Debbie Hansen enjoy a sunny day after harvest in Cougar Hills Vineyard, where Dave farms the vineyards while Debbie produces the wines. The wind machine in the background protects the vineyard from frost.

Bottom: Cabernet franc, one of the classic Bordeaux varietals, has become a prominent attraction in the tasting room. Since its first release in 2001, the high-scoring wine has become one of the signature wines of Cougar Crest.

Facing page: The dormant vines of Cougar Hills Vineyard, brown and hardened off, are ready for the cold blast of winter that seems so far away on a sunny day.
Photographs by Andréa Johnson

Located on three acres seven miles west of Walla Walla, the 2006-built winery building represents the culmination of a decade of planning. Rastra blocks, made from recycled polystyrene mixed with concrete, were chosen for construction of the walls. Sustainable, green features such as tankless hot water heaters, heat pumps, steam cleaners, recycled steel wall studs, low-e windows, and subterranean library wine storage minimize the environmental impact of the winery operations.

Estate vineyards have been the key to quality and consistency in Cougar Crest wines over the years. Living in the vineyards, watching the weather, and observing the vines daily assures year-round control of the grapes from the ground up. Wind-blown loess, silt loam, gravelly layers, and veins of river rock from the prehistoric meanderings of the Walla Walla River provide a variety of soil types that can be tasted in the wine. The unique wines made from these different vineyard sites give Deborah a palette of options for creating single-vineyard wines or complex blends.

Top: The production facility at Cougar Crest, where grapes from the estate vineyards arrive, are made into wine, and are bottled, all under the same roof.

Bottom: Glowing lights of the tasting room warm the twilight sky. The Prairie-style architecture, with its low-slung roof line and square shapes, blends well with the rolling hills of Walla Walla.

Facing page: Open-beam construction, rich vineyard colors, and plenty of natural light connect the tasting room to the great outdoors. Wide vistas of open farmland and vibrant sunsets surround the winery.
Photographs by Andréa Johnson

Viognier

Pair with seared scallops with a reduction sauce of viognier, papaya, and ground coriander.

Merlot

Pair with lamb chops with a reduction sauce of merlot, rosemary, and bay leaf.

Port

Pair with chocolate brownie topped with black cherries simmered in port reduction with nutmeg.

Tastings

Walla Walla Tasting Room: Open to the public daily, year-round
Woodinville Tasting Room: Open to the public Thursday through Monday
Spokane Tasting Room: Open to the public Wednesday through Monday

Watch a video of winemaker Deborah Hansen leading a tour through the apple orchards and Cougar Hills Vineyard, one of the family's estate vineyards.

Cougar Crest
ESTATE WINERY

2009
CABERNET FRANC
estate grown

walla walla valley

Desert Wind Winery

Prosser

Just one visit to the namesake vineyard for Desert Wind Winery and it's immediately evident why the particular name was chosen. Located in the Wahluke Slope appellation in eastern Washington, the area is known for its extreme summer conditions and minimal annual rainfall.

While at first glance the environment doesn't seem favorable to grape-growing, the Fries and Jenkins families have established two estate vineyards—Desert Wind and Sacagawea—that produce such tremendous fruit that they were inspired to open a winery in Washington. Taking notes from what works in their Oregon winery, Duck Pond Cellars, the families founded the Desert Wind label in 2001, followed by a production facility in 2004 and a Prosser tasting room in 2007.

Nearly 15 varietals of wine fall under the Desert Wind label, with a Bordeaux-inspired red blend, called Ruah, as the flagship wine. Meaning wind, breath, or spirit in Hebrew, Ruah is full-bodied with a lush core of concentrated blackberry fruit and a hint of anise on the palate. Underlying all of the wines is the focus on producing premium wines at affordable prices, possible because of the use of all estate-grown fruit and the involvement of numerous family members.

The winery's architecture captures the Southwest essence and blends perfectly with the barren landscape. Visitors can enjoy the varietals in the tasting room, open daily, or schedule a tour of the facility. In addition to the winemaking facility and tasting room, the winery also houses a gourmet marketplace, an event facility, a restaurant, and four luxurious guest rooms—all expanding on the idea of an elegant desert retreat.

Top: Inspired by the spirit of Santa Fe, Desert Wind's Southwest-inspired facility lies on a bluff overlooking the Yakima River.

Bottom: The Desert Wind tasting room is open daily and offers visitors a selection of estate-grown wines, as well as gourmet food, upscale home décor, and unique gifts.

Facing page: Inside the winery, MOJAVE at Desert Wind offers upscale wine country cuisine using Northwest ingredients with a unique Southwestern twist.
Photographs by Andréa Johnson

Doubleback

Walla Walla

For former NFL Quarterback Drew Bledsoe, owning a winery has been a longtime aspiration that would allow him to combine his passion for fine wine and love of the Walla Walla Valley. Drew returned to his hometown in 2007 after his retirement from the NFL to plant his estate vineyard, McQueen. In 2008, he launched Doubleback, an estate-focused winery with a goal of producing ultra-premium cabernet sauvignon from the Walla Walla Valley AVA. To make this dream a reality, Drew hired his childhood friend Chris Figgins of Leonetti Cellar as his consulting winemaker. Together they have a true collaboration from dirt to bottle as Chris consults on all winemaking and viticulture practices; he also assisted in the vineyard design and planting for McQueen.

In early 2011, Drew acquired a second estate vineyard which he named Bob Healy, after his late father-in-law, to continue cultivating premium Walla Walla Valley fruit for Doubleback. Both vineyards follow VINEA farming guidelines of sustainability. Drew and his wife Maura are committed to creating a premium wine experience that is completely focused on quality, using only the best viticulture and winemaking practices to ensure that Doubleback will be one of the best bottles of wine ever tasted.

Top: Drew and Maura Bledsoe in McQueen Vineyard.

Bottom: Bob Healy Vineyard.

Facing page: McQueen Vineyard with views of the Walla Walla Valley.
Photographs by Andréa Johnson

Dunham Cellars
Walla Walla

When visitors enjoy a tasting flight at Dunham Cellars' Hangar Lounge, the word "flight" takes on a whole new meaning. Located in a beautifully remodeled World War II-era airplane hangar at the Walla Walla airport, Dunham provides not only award-winning wines but also a unique experience. Owners Mike and Joanne Dunham and their son, senior winemaker Eric Dunham, have built a welcoming, friendly atmosphere that allows the wine to become more than just something to drink—it's a multifaceted experience that augments food, art, music, and, most importantly, life.

Since its first vintage in 1995, Dunham has simply taken off, with its wines receiving not only local acclaim but national and international attention as well. Numerous vintages have been granted scores in the 90s by *Wine Enthusiast* and *Wine Spectator*. Even more impressive, the winery has also been designated by the Wall Street Journal multiple years in a row as producing the best American syrah. In addition to the syrah, the winery's portfolio includes cabernet sauvignon, merlot, riesling, chardonnay, red table wine, and a Bordeaux-style blend.

Of particular note is the Shirley Mays Chardonnay, which is dedicated to Eric's grandmother and features labels that tell inspirational stories of those who have been affected by breast cancer. Dunham proudly supports the Puget Sound affiliate of Susan G. Komen for the Cure in the hope that one day there will be a cure; it is a perfect example of the family's passion for life.

Top: The well-worn path to the tasting room is highlighted by glass artist Lee Proctor's magnificent bronze art, *Waterfall*.

Bottom: Mike and Joanne Dunham relax with their two loyal winery dogs, Maysy and Konnie.

Facing page: A Walla Walla vineyard enjoys picturesque views of Blue Mountains in the background.
Photographs by Andrëa Johnson

The fruit and the vineyards in which they grow are incredibly crucial to the development of Dunham Cellars' consistent, elegant wines. Paying great attention to growing practices—including sustainability to ensure present needs are met without compromising future generations—has always been a focus at Dunham.

Working closely with their farming company, Appellation Management Group, Eric and winemaker Dan Wampfler select only the finest grapes from several renowned estate vineyards in the Walla Walla Valley and Columbia Valley appellations. One of the winery's largest vineyards is Lewis Estate Vineyard, located north of Prosser on Rattlesnake Ridge, where the fruit is so remarkable that Eric and his team deemed it worthy of Dunham's first vineyard-designated wine. Located in the Blue Mountain foothills east of Walla Walla, Kenny Hill Vineyard is the newest addition to Dunham's sources. It is one of the first dry land vineyards planted in the northwest.

No less important than the high quality of fruit sourced from the best vineyards is the passion and knowledge of the winery's team, which ensures achievement of the lofty goal of creating age-worthy, yet presently approachable, wines. A true family endeavor, Dunham Cellars is a collaboration of incredible talents. Mike's business acumen and Joanne's creative genius lay the foundation. Rounding out the genius is Eric's lifelong interest in winemaking—which was sparked at an early age, as wine played a role in every family dinner. And the rest of the team is truly indispensable, sharing in the belief that wine can bring people together when crafted and presented correctly.

Left: The Hangar Lounge is the social hub of Dunham Cellars and a great place to have a memorable event.
Photograph by Andréa Johnson

Eric and Dan—whose résumé includes a position as research winemaker at Ste. Michelle Wine Estates—follow a winemaking philosophy that they explain as a minimalist approach. They know when to leave the wine alone, providing just enough gentle treatment at the right time to craft varietals they are proud to have under the Dunham label.

Visiting the winery only serves to enhance the experience. Through offering guided tours of the winery and tastings in the lounge, the family and staff enjoy their favorite part of being involved with Dunham: a chance to interact with a variety of people and share their creations that elevate wine to an entirely new level.

Above: The Dunham Cellars winemaking team, Eric Dunham and Dan Wampfler, taste the next vintage.
Photograph by Todd Tucker

Left: Dunham Cellars is proud to support Susan G. Komen for the Cure, in memory of Mike's mother, Shirley Mays Dunham.
Photograph by Andréa Johnson

Facing page: The garden patio is a wonderful place for picnicking and enjoying a glass of wine.
Photograph by Andréa Johnson

Columbia Valley Syrah
Pair with pork tenderloin wrapped in prosciutto and drizzled with a habanero-plum glaze.

Cabernet Sauvignon
Exquisite with a New York strip steak.

Riesling
Perfect with a spicy Thai dish.

Tastings
Open daily, year-round

Visit Dunham Cellars' website.

FIGGINS
Walla Walla

For Chris Figgins and his family, FIGGINS is a culmination of many years of vision and dedication to produce a site-specific wine from the Walla Walla Valley. FIGGINS is an estate-grown, single-vineyard, Bordeaux varietal blend sourced solely from the 32-acre Figgins Estate Vineyard site in the Walla Walla Valley and produced in very small quantities.

FIGGINS was born from the site, with great consideration given to planting the proper varietals, placement within the vineyard, trellising, and the hundreds of other decisions that go into winegrowing with the ultimate goal to elevate the site through the wine. With winemaking in his blood—Chris' parents Gary and Nancy Figgins founded Leonetti Cellar in 1977—Chris is a second-generation winemaker and has been on a lifelong quest to find the perfect vineyard site to honor his past and further his family's legacy.

Sloping south-southwest from 1,750 to 1,500 feet, Figgins Estate Vineyard lies in the foothills of the Blue Mountains at the northeast end of Walla Walla Valley. The 60-acre estate's location, aspect, elevation, and very deep silt loam soil make it ideal vineyard land and, essentially, Chris' dream site. An integral part of the family's process, VINEA Winegrowers' Sustainable Trust practices are employed throughout, ensuring the land is well taken care of.

Planted with cabernet sauvignon, petit verdot, merlot, and a very small block of riesling, the vineyard produces an incredible single-vineyard Bordeaux blend and a very dry riesling. FIGGINS is an enormously gratifying addition under Figgins Family Wine Estates and perfectly complements the fine portfolio of wines from Leonetti Cellar.

Top: The stunning views of the Blue Mountains from atop the Figgins Estate Vineyard.

Middle: The Shouting Stone block is planted to high density on a low cordon wire, much like it would be in Bordeaux.

Bottom: The FIGGINS name represents quality and a dedication to the land.

Facing page: The end posts from the block are old limestone fence posts from Kansas, very near where the Figgins family first settled.
Photographs by Andréa Johnson

Force Majeure Vineyards

Red Mountain

Force Majeure, French for "superior force", is a term used to describe the relentless, powerful forces of nature that formed the terroir of the winery's Red Mountain vineyards. Founders Paul McBride and Ryan Johnson approach wine with the philosophy that great wine is created in the vineyard. Their goal is to take meticulously farmed fruit and combine it with top winemakers in Washington State to create artisanal wines that capture the pinnacle of Red Mountain terroir and winemaking prowess.

For nearly a decade after relocating to the area, Paul's entrepreneurial interests became increasingly sparked by the potential to create world-class wines from Washington. Ryan was well-established as the vineyard manager at Ciel du Cheval, Cadence Cara Mia, Galitzine Estate, and DeLille Grand Ciel vineyards, all located within Washington's famed Red Mountain AVA. When the two met, it became immediately obvious they shared a passion to improve on the state's already exquisite wines, and they determined to vault its quality to rival the best in the world.

The resulting portfolio of Force Majeure Vineyards, originally called Grand Rêve Vintners, is the pinnacle of six accomplished winemakers embarking on the creation of six unique wines. Utilizing premium fruit hand-cultivated and selected by Ryan, this all-star ensemble crafts limited production wines that are available through the winery's registry and at select retailers and restaurants. This vintner dream team includes Ben Smith of Cadence, Ross Mickel of Ross Andrew Winery, Mark McNeilly of Mark Ryan Winery, Carolyn Lakewold of Donedei, Chris Gorman of Gorman Winery, and James Mantone of Syncline. With uncompromising attention to winemaking detail and progressive viticulture practices, the acclaimed series sets new benchmarks for quality across multiple varietals.

Top: A winding road leads to the multiple elevations and terroir of the unique Red Mountain site.

Bottom: The passion and care taken in the vineyards is what sets Force Majeure apart.

Facing page: Sweeping views from Red Mountain's highest vines: the upper syrah block of Force Majeure Vineyards.
Photographs by Andréa Johnson

This impressive culmination of experienced winemakers is certainly something to be proud of, but ultimately it's the passion and care taken in the vineyards that sets Force Majeure Vineyards apart. Inspired by the vineyards of Hermitage, Priorat, and Côte Rôtie in France, Paul and Ryan challenged existing viticulture practices and embarked on an ambitious plan to plant a vineyard on the steep, rocky hillside of Red Mountain. Development began in 2004 and spanned seven years. The Herculean effort involved carefully matching clonal varietals to the nine distinct soil types found on the site's twisting blocks formed from ancient floods and volcanic activity. Because of the rough, rocky nature of the acreage and elevations ranging from 960 to 1,230 feet, mechanization is virtually impossible, so everything is accomplished by hand. This extreme viticulture has led Paul, Ryan, and their crew to give some areas irreverent nicknames like El Terror and The Devil's Playground.

In 2011, Ryan and Paul added to their vineyard portfolio a 20-acre site christened Parabellum Vineyard, after the multiple gun casings found scattered on the site. This expansion affirms their commitment to Red Mountain and their ongoing passion to establish Washington among the great wine regions of the world.

Left: Paul McBride shares his passion for Washington wine and viticulture from the Kirkland tasting room.

Facing page: The steep canvas of Ryan Johnson's 40-acre art project.
Photographs by Andréa Johnson

WINE & FARE

Viognier
Pair with Asian salad and shellfish.

Ptera
Delicious with savory barbecue, grilled ribeye, or smoked duck confit.

Syrah
Excellent with pan-seared foie gras and herb-grilled Portobello mushrooms.

Tastings
By appointment only

FORCE
Majeure

Goose Ridge Vineyards and Estate Winery

Richland

F or the Monson family, breaking into the wine industry was an easy transition, considering the family's longtime involvement in diversified agriculture. In the cattle business since the 1940s, the Monsons began thinking about further diversification for the family's business. Yet growing grapes wasn't even considered until Dr. Walter Clore, known as the father of the Washington wine industry, showed up on the family's doorstep talking about how the area—and their land in particular—was one of the premier sites in the state for growing wine grapes. He certainly convinced them, and by 1998 the Monsons, with Walter's help, established the vineyard, naming it after Goose Gap and the area's popularity as a stopping point for migrating geese. The winery's opening followed just one year later.

Today Goose Ridge Vineyards and Estate Winery is still family-owned and operated, focusing on a limited production of wines from estate-grown grapes. Visionary owners Arvid and Suzanne Monson, along with their children Valerie, Bill, and Molly, stay true to the original reason for starting Goose Ridge: the land. The viticulture practices and site selection take great precedence, as winemaker Kendall Mix works closely with vineyard manager Robert Rivera and CFO Glen Ward to identify the best blocks for each varietal on the 1,600-acre vineyard.

Top: Goose Ridge believes that great wines begin in the vineyard. For that reason, blocks of fruit are selected for their exceptional character and complexity.

Bottom: Committed to sound viticultural practices, vineyard manager Robert Rivera works diligently to ensure consistent fruit quality, vintage to vintage.

Facing page: Located in the Columbia Valley, the Monson family founded Goose Ridge Vineyards and Estate Winery in 1998.
Photographs by Andréa Johnson

Exquisite Bordeaux and Rhône varietals are Goose Ridge's specialty, with plenty of options both in single varietals—cabernet sauvignon, merlot, syrah, chardonnay, pinot gris, and riesling—and three blends. Goose Ridge is especially known for its signature blend, Vireo, which is named after the songbirds that are all over the vineyards. This blend was inspired by a wine sampled in Australia that the family fell in love with. Another special blend is Sol Duc, a Meritage blend named after the sparkling waters that nourish the sun-drenched Columbia Valley. Both consistently have scored 90-plus points. The third blend is g3, which stands for the third generation which expanded the family business into the wine industry.

The family spirit truly shines in Goose Ridge's Woodinville Tasting Room, as well as the Richland Tasting Room and Event Center, which is located in the heart of the vineyard, just a short distance from Red Mountain. Picnic grounds, a large indoor event space, and beautiful native landscaping are perfect complements to the Richland building's European yet native flair. And the fact that the wines are approachable, everyone is extremely friendly, and the setting is simply breathtaking creates an atmosphere where guests can relax and enjoy the unbelievable quality and care that goes into every bottle.

Top: With more than two decades of experience, winemaker Kendall Mix handcrafts limited quantities of exquisite wines with uncompromising varietal expression and quality.
Photograph by Andréa Johnson

Bottom: Two patios, four regulation-size bocce courts, and three acres of manicured lawn surrounded by vineyards makes a perfect winery getaway.
Photograph by Andréa Johnson

Facing page: With a foundation of family tradition, a reflection of hard work, and a commitment to quality, the Monson family has been farming the Columbia Valley for more than 50 years.
Photograph by Bill Watts

WINE & FARE

Vireo
Exceptional with slowly roasted braised lamb shanks
with merguez tomato sauce and chickpeas.

Syrah
Wonderful with pancetta-wrapped quail with sage risotto
and butternut squash confit.

Cabernet
Lovely with Stilton- and wild mushroom-stuffed Chateaubriand in a
balsamic jus with roasted garlic and rosemary-studded mashed potatoes.

Pinot Gris
Perfect with nori-dusted ahi tuna with Asian arancini
and silky wasabi sauce.

Tastings
Open to the public daily, year-round
Also available at tasting room, Woodinville

GOOSE RIDGE
ESTATE WINERY

Guardian Cellars
Woodinville

The Alibi, Chalk Line, The Wanted, Gun Metal, Confidential Source, and Five-0. These sound like something from a crime novel, yet they're actually the names of Guardian Cellars' award-winning wines. With a hint of playfulness, these wines perfectly express the background and lively personalities of Guardian's founders, Jerry Riener and his wife Jennifer Sullivan.

On his way to work as a police officer, Jerry often drove past Woodinville's wineries. One day, his natural curiosity got the better of him, and he stopped to check out a building that was hopping with activity. Upon walking inside, Jerry realized he was somewhere he had never been before—a winery. The crew at Matthews Cellars was in the process of bottling, so Jerry jumped in to lend a hand. A month later, Jerry was back at it as a "cellar rat" for harvest.

Jerry quickly became a fixture at the winery, regularly volunteering 40 hours a week. With his University of Washington chemistry degree in hand, Jerry found himself doing everything from laboratory work to punch downs to sales. While at Matthews, Jerry became friends with budding winemaker Mark McNeilly. Jerry soon started volunteering fulltime at Mark's winery, Mark Ryan Winery. Jerry and Mark grew Mark Ryan Winery together, until Mark helped Jerry create Guardian Cellars in 2004.

From its beginnings with 2004 Gun Metal, a Bordeaux blend hailing from Columbia Valley's Connor Lee Vineyard, Guardian Cellars' focus has been on using the state's finest grapes and spectacular new French oak to create fun and approachable wines. Since those early days, Jerry has expanded into some of the state's other top vineyards, including Klipsun, Stillwater Creek, Ciel du Cheval, and Stone Tree. Guardian's portfolio has grown to include

Top: Guardian Cellars' wines: 10 bold reds and a gorgeous sauvignon blanc.
Photograph by Andréa Johnson

Bottom: Winemaker Jerry Riener and his wife, Jennifer Sullivan, in the Guardian Cellars tasting room.
Photograph by Andréa Johnson

Facing page: Bordeaux blends Gun Metal and The Wanted are so delicious it's almost criminal.
Photograph by Keith Megay

a lineup of nine delicious wines, featuring names inspired by Jerry and Jennifer's day jobs of police officer and newspaper reporter. Today their offerings include Bordeaux blends from four different vineyards, as well as a Red Mountain cabernet, a syrah, a table wine, and one white. Jerry's winemaking philosophy is simple: every bottle must represent a blend of art and science.

Jerry and Jennifer adore showing off the winery to everyone who visits. On any Saturday or Sunday, visitors are greeted by an atmosphere of great music, rock posters, and modern furniture. The couple welcomes questions and loves to give tours of the production facility. Step through the warehouse doors, and you'll be whisked into a production facility full of new French oak barrels and shiny winemaking equipment. What sets Guardian Cellars apart is, without question, Jerry and Jennifer's gregarious, fun-loving personalities.

Above: Jerry crushing grapes on a sunny harvest day.
Photograph by Mike Siegel

Left: The lineup: Angel, Chalk Line, and Gun Metal.
Photograph by Mike Siegel

Facing page: Ripped from the headlines: Officer Jerry and reporter Jennifer at the winery.
Photograph by Andréa Johnson

Gun Metal
Excellent with pan-seared ribeye with porcini, rosemary, and smoked salt rub.

Angel
Pair with seared scallops on citrus, arugula, and pomegranate salad.

The Informant
Delicious with lamb chops.

Chalk Line
Luscious with comfort food, such as Jerry's favorite of tater-tot casserole or Jennifer's favorite of pizza.

Tastings
Open to the public Saturday and Sunday

Watch a video of Jerry Riener discussing how he went from a police officer to owner and winemaker of Guardian Cellars.

2009

GUARDIAN

Gun Metal

CONNER LEE VINEYARD

Karma Vineyards
Chelan

V isiting Karma Vineyards is an experience like none other. The true family atmosphere is refreshing, the wines are sensational, and the wine cave and restaurant are not to be missed.

The thread of family is woven throughout every part of the winery. Owners Julie and Bret Pittsinger originally arrived at the idea of a winery because it satisfied not only their own interest in wine but also their desire to provide an agricultural lifestyle for their children, which would show them the value of hard work. Upon founding the winery in 2007, Julie and Bret arrived at the moniker Karma, an interesting meaning in itself but also a clever combination of their children's names: Karle and Matthew.

In addition to its portfolio of numerous varietals such as syrah and pinot noir, Karma is especially known for its sparkling wine. Since its founding, Karma has been one of the few producers in Washington State to follow the laborious, traditional method—called méthode champenoise—used in France's Champagne region. The exceptional offering is a bubbly, crisp, dry wine with aromas of vanilla and Granny Smith apples, crafted from chardonnay and pinot noir grapes grown on the estate.

Not content to simply stick with what they know, Julie and Bret are always looking for ways to improve and expand. They are currently preparing to offer a brandy—aged nearly seven years in the barrel—as well as open a distillery.

Top: Karma Vineyards' Méthode Champenoise.
Photograph by Mollie Nickles

Bottom: The koi pond off the Karma patio.
Photograph by Andréa Johnson

Facing page: Karma Vineyards.
Photograph by Andréa Johnson

Also on Karma's property, on the impressive south shore of Lake Chelan, lie nearly 14 acres of vineyards. Sustainable methods, including a custom compost tea, allow Julie and Bret to maintain the overall long-term health of the vineyards.

In keeping with the magnificent agricultural feel of the area, Julie and Bret built the winery as an underground wine cave, ensuring minimal affect to the neighborhood and surrounding vineyards. The 3,000-square-foot facility, which perhaps should be more accurately referred to as a cavern given its spaciousness, naturally maintains an ideal temperature of 55 degrees. Its beauty has become quite a draw for tours as well as for couples who are tying the knot.

The onsite restaurant, named 18 Brix, is a reference to the low sugar—or brix—levels at which champagne grapes are typically harvested. The landscaped patio is an excellent spot to enjoy wine and fare during the spring, summer, and fall, as koi swim in the adjacent pond. In the winter, the cozy fireplace evokes the essence that Julie and Bret strive to spread throughout the winery: elegance with a touch of humor.

Top: Karma's estate gewürztraminer vineyard.
Photograph by Jacqueline Brynn

Middle: The door leading to the underground wine cave.
Photograph by Jacqueline Brynn

Bottom: Inside the Karma cave.
Photograph by Ron Miller

Facing page: Karma Vineyards' tasting room.
Photograph by Jacqueline Brynn

WINE & FARE

Chardonnay
Perfect with clams steamed in wine, garlic, and butter.

Zen
Excellent with a filet mignon topped with a Zen demiglace.

Estate Gewürztraminer
Wonderful with sweet potato fries.

Tastings
Open to the public, year round

Kiona Vineyards and Winery

Benton City

Kiona Vineyards and Winery is one of the oldest family-owned and -operated wineries in the state of Washington. It all began with John Williams in 1975, when he and a friend planted the first vineyard on Red Mountain, located at the convergence of the Yakima and Columbia Valleys in southeastern Washington. John's son Scott and his siblings planted Kiona's estate vineyard under their father's guidance, leading to the winery's first commercial vintage in 1980. When he was young, Scott was interested in the family business but decided that making a living might be easier with a degree in engineering. The vines kept calling to him, however, and he jumped at the opportunity to help pioneer the emerging Washington wine industry.

Nestled on the south slope of Red Mountain above the Yakima River, Kiona's estate vineyard sits on 84 acres of some of the driest land in the state, receiving less than six inches of rain year-round. The harsh environment results in very intense and concentrated fruit, creating a distinct taste. The grapes tend to have tough skins, small berries, and complex character. Temperature swings allow for higher concentration of sugar and acidity, furthering the distinctiveness of Red Mountain fruit.

Scott finds solace in winemaking, learning much from his father and watching his son JJ follow in the family path as the winery's sales representative and marketing manager. It's a rare occurrence in this day and age for children to be interested in the same thing as their parents, so Scott takes great pride that three generations are now involved.

Top: Scott Williams grows the grapes and makes the wine for Kiona Vineyards and Winery, a rare occurrence in the modern wine industry.

Bottom: Employing both American and French oak, all of the red wines at Kiona Vineyards and Winery are aged in traditional 60-gallon barrels.

Facing page: Form meets function at Kiona Vineyards and Winery's impressive new building. The 20,000-square-foot facility houses the tasting room and barrel storage.
Photographs by Andréa Johnson

The winery's tasting room was housed for many years in the basement of John and his wife Ann's house. In 2007, a new tasting room and barrel cellar was opened. Built of steel and concrete to withstand the elements, the building's clean lines, playful geometric shapes, and vaulted wood ceilings frame an array of glass walls with panoramic views of vineyards, mountains, and sky.

Interestingly, Kiona Vineyards and Winery was the first winery in the United States to introduce the rare Eastern European varietal Lemberger, which Scott emphasizes as a palate-pleaser and well-suited for all dishes. In fact, Kiona's Estate Lemberger recently earned a best-in-show award in Hong Kong for Shanghainese cuisine.

Accolades, which have been abundant, are a confirmation of Kiona Vineyards and Winery's excellence. However, Scott looks to his customers for confirmation of his wines' quality. His family knows they are responsible for the wines from start to finish and ensure that the taster gets a good sense of their land and traditions with the first glass.

Top: Eastern Washington's arid landscape is perfect for growing quality wine grapes. The Kiona Estate vineyard was the first planted on Red Mountain.

Bottom: With 300 days of sunshine and less than six inches of rain a year, the Red Mountain AVA is always a great place to visit with friends and family.

Facing page: The sign, with Red Mountain in the background, has welcomed tasters to the premises of Kiona Vineyards and Winery since 1983.
Photographs by Andréa Johnson

Estate Red Mountain Lemberger
Ideal with soups, salads, pasta, and salmon.

Estate Red Mountain Cabernet Sauvignon
Pair with roasted leg of lamb and mint chutney or a hearty cut of beef.

Late Harvest Riesling
Delectable with Tex-Mex or Chinese food.

Estate Red Mountain Big Kiona Zinfandel
Incredible with turkey, quail, or steak.

Tastings
Open daily to the public

Watch a video of owner Scott Williams discussing the beautiful site and unique history of Kiona Vineyards and Winery.

L'Ecole Nº 41

Walla Walla Valley

A 1915 classic schoolhouse stands tall in Lowden, a small community just west of Walla Walla. It is home to L'Ecole Nº 41, and its former classrooms are the hub of this third-generation, family-owned artisan winery. Led by owner and managing winemaker Marty Clubb, L'Ecole's wines are prized for their richness and complexity, vintage after vintage. Founded in 1983, its first merlot brought attention to the winery, and today its cabernet sauvignon-based blends and sémillon are equally sought after.

As a traditional brick and mortar winery, L'Ecole is engaged in growing and making all of its wines. In addition to the winery's Walla Walla Valley estate vineyards, Marty has developed longterm relationships with some of the most prestigious, mature vineyards in Washington, providing a foundation for quality and consistency throughout the entire lineup of wines.

L'Ecole's portfolio is divided into two distinct offerings, the Walla Walla Valley and Columbia Valley collections. The Walla Walla wines are primarily single-vineyard and terroir-driven, reflecting the unmistakable typicity of each vineyard site, all certified sustainable and Salmon-Safe. With increasing vine maturity and precision viticulture practices, these wines—such as the Estate Perigee from Seven Hills Vineyard, a highly acclaimed signature red blend—are known for refined elegance, structure, and complexity.

The Columbia Valley wines, all with a varietal focus, are the cornerstone of the portfolio. They are crafted from older, proven vineyards, many planted in the 1970s and early 1980s. Working alongside the state's finest growers, Marty's intent is to showcase the best expression of a particular varietal—all with L'Ecole's hallmark style.

Top: Marty Clubb takes great pride in being the owner and managing winemaker at L'Ecole Nº 41.
Photograph by Kirk Hirota

Bottom: The Estate Perigee from Seven Hills Vineyard is L'Ecole's highly acclaimed signature red blend.
Photograph by Kirk Hirota

Facing page: Estate Seven Hills Vineyard was established as one of Walla Walla Valley's oldest and most prestigious vineyards.
Photograph by Andréa Johnson

Given Marty's dedication to state-of-the-art vineyard practices and traditional winemaking, it is no surprise *Wine & Spirits* magazine has honored L'Ecole as a winery of the year for 10 consecutive years. It is one of only 26 wineries from around the world with this 10-year distinction in *Wine & Spirits'* prestigious hall of fame.

L'Ecole's high-quality wines have earned a loyal following, but the charm of the winery's turn-of-the-century Frenchtown schoolhouse—featuring many original details—is not to be missed. Guests are welcome year-round, and the winery also offers a seasonal, reservation-only tasting and production tour held in the winery's cellar where a restored, hand-painted mural of a children's Christmas pageant and the original children's water fountain are located. This unique experience offers visitors an insider's view of the winery and an opportunity to sample library, limited production, and reserve wines.

L'Ecole has been Instrumental in establishing Walla Walla as one of the most exciting viticultural regions in America. As the third winery in the Walla Walla Valley and the 20th in the state, its experience and innovation reflect an ardent pioneering spirit, much like the French-Canadians who settled the area and made wine during the early 1800s. The name L'Ecole N° 41, French for "the school" located in district 41, was chosen to honor this rich heritage.

Above Left: L'Ecole N° 41 is located in a historic Frenchtown schoolhouse built in 1915.
Photograph by Andréa Johnson

Top: L'Ecole N° 41 tasting room provides a welcoming ambience to sample various vintages.
Photograph by Andréa Johnson

Bottom: Marty Clubb and his son Riley represent the second and third generations of the family-owned winery.
Photograph by Andréa Johnson

Facing page: The elegant wines of L'Ecole are showcased in the beautifully restored tasting room.
Photograph by Kirk Hirota

WINE & FARE

Sémillon
Pair with seared sea scallops
with Walla Walla sweet onion-apricot compote.

Cabernet Sauvignon
Delicious with medallions of beef tenderloin
with chanterelle mushroom ragout.

Estate Merlot
Wonderful with duck breast drizzled with a cherry and merlot demiglace.

Estate Perigee
Great with steak au poivre with brandy cream sauce.

Tastings
Open to the public daily, year-round

Watch a video of owner and managing winemaker
Marty Clubb discussing L'Ecole N° 41 and
its Seven Hills Vineyard.

L'Ecole
N° 41

WALLA WALLA VALLEY

Leonetti Cellar
Walla Walla

For more than 30 years, the Figgins family has been producing wines of consistently high quality at Leonetti Cellar. What started as a dream to make world-class wines in Walla Walla has turned out to be a true success story, as today Leonetti produces some of the most sought-after American wines in the world.

Gary Figgins' first exposure to the world of wine came as a child when his maternal grandparents, immigrants from Italy who settled in the Walla Walla Valley in 1902, served him small portions of diluted wine produced in their dirt-floored cellar. Frank and Rose Leonetti never conceived that years later, these first "hints" of wine would inspire the creation of a world-class winery.

Completely self-educated in the art of making wine, Gary discovered a further passion for wine as a young father and Army reservist training in Northern California. Side trips to California's wine country inspired Gary to begin making wines at home. In the beginning, he fermented numerous fruits and berries from the bountiful Walla Walla Valley, with varying degrees of success. Soon Gary's entrance into wine production would come full circle when, in 1974, he and his uncles planted an acre of cabernet sauvignon and a bit of white riesling on the hillside above the original Leonetti homestead.

After several years honing his skills as an amateur winemaker, Gary and his wife, Nancy, bonded Leonetti in 1977 and produced its first wines a year later. What his early wines lacked in quantity—produced in a tiny cellar beneath his home—they made up for in quality. Gary and Nancy soon realized they were on to something when demand quickly outgrew the modest production.

Top: Old Stone Winery doors open for a private event.
Photograph by Andréa Johnson

Bottom: Leonetti's iconic label.
Photograph by Tim Hall

Facing page: The late summer sun sets over the Walla Walla Valley and Loess Vineyard.
Photograph by Andréa Johnson

Having grown up immersed in the business, Gary and Nancy's son, Chris, joined the winery fulltime in 1996 after receiving a degree in horticulture from Washington State University. After many years of mentoring under his father, Chris now leads the next generation at the helm of Figgins Family Wine Estates, where he continues to pursue world-class wines of true distinction.

In early 2007, Amy Figgins joined her brother Chris to further assist at Leonetti Cellar. Today both Chris and Amy work hard to reflect the deep sense of place that daily inspires the Figgins family, while staying true to their winemaking philosophy of maintaining complete control over the process from start to finish. Together, these elements allow the Figgins to produce some of the world's finest varietal wines—cabernet sauvignon, merlot, and sangiovese—that accurately reflect the terroir of their Walla Walla Valley vineyards. It is clear that no effort or expense is spared in pursuing meticulous, sustainable viticulture and winemaking in their vineyards and state-of-the-art winery.

Top: The sun rises over Loess Vineyard at the Leonetti Cellar estate.

Bottom: Two generations of winemakers are focused on producing world-class wines from the Walla Walla Valley.

Facing page: Constructed to honor the fine architecture and craftsman materials of the past, the production facility is built with an eye to the future, fully embracing modern winemaking to elevate viticultural efforts.
Photographs by Andrèa Johnson

WINE & FARE

Leonetti Cellar Sangiovese
Pair with pasta or salmon.

Leonetti Cellar Merlot
Exquisite with quail or pork.

Leonetti Cellar Cabernet Sauvignon
Stellar with beef or lamb.

Leonetti Reserve
Delicious with chocolate or decadent dessert.

Tastings
Closed to the public

Leonetti Cellar

Long Shadows Vintners

Walla Walla

Long Shadows Vintners is the creation of Washington wine legend Allen Shoup. Founded by Allen in 2003 following a 20-year career leading Chateau Ste. Michelle and its affiliate wineries, Long Shadows brings together seven internationally acclaimed winemakers who are partners in a winery dedicated to each crafting a single, distinct world-class wine showcasing the exceptional grapes of the Columbia Valley.

Widely recognized as a founding father of Washington's wine industry, Allen's lifelong ambition has been to elevate and shape the state's reputation for outstanding wines. Recognizing that the world's newest and arguably most unique wine region was capable of growing wine grapes that would compete with the finest in the world, Allen also knew the region lacked the knowledge that multigenerational winemakers bring from experience spanning centuries. While CEO at Chateau Ste. Michelle, Allen helped compensate for this by establishing two international partnerships with world-renowned vintners, first with Italy's Piero Antinori to craft Col Solare and then with Ernst Loosen to make Eroica Riesling. Long Shadows is an extension of this work and a natural outgrowth of his friendships with many of the world's great winemakers built over three decades in the industry.

As these notable winemakers came to visit the Columbia Valley with Allen, they began to catch his enthusiasm for the growing region and his dream of a winery encompassing multiple winemakers—each an owner-partner crafting a single, unique wine—began to unfold. The partner list at Long Shadows reads like a who's who of the wine industry—all known for creating benchmark wines. Randy Dunn crafts Feather, an intense and elegant cabernet sauvignon. John Duval creates Sequel, a deep, dark syrah. Pirouette, a red blend

Top: Long Shadows Vintners is a continuation of Allen Shoup's lifelong ambition to shine an international spotlight on all that Washington wines have to offer.

Bottom: Chester-Kidder, named after Allen's mother and grandmother, is a gorgeous red wine blend and one of seven wines in the Long Shadows portfolio, each a stand-alone wine crafted by a distinct, world-class vintner.

Facing page: Long Shadows founder Allen Shoup and a group of investors purchased The Benches, a spectacular vineyard rising 1,350 feet above sea level at its crown and dropping more than 1,000 feet to the edge of the Columbia River, to provide a long-term source for top quality grapes.
Photographs by Andréa Johnson

that is bursting with complex aromas and flavors, is a collaboration between Agustin Huneeus Sr. and Philippe Melka. Then there's a merlot with a silky and prolonged finish named Pedestal, crafted by Michel Rolland, while Armin Diel's Poet's Leap is an off dry riesling with welcoming richness. Another red blend, full of complexity and flavor, is Saggi, the brainchild of father-son duo Ambrogio and Giovanni Folonari. Gilles Nicault, who is Long Shadows' head winemaker overseeing daily winemaking, perfects Chester-Kidder, an excellent red blend beautifully integrated around a spicy core.

Allen's unique model specified that the winemakers would return to Washington each vintage to guide fruit selection, blending, and the wine's release. This necessitated an on-site head winemaker capable of coordinating the day-to-day operations with the partners, which he found in Gilles. By 2004, the first vintage was released—a 2003 riesling—with the first red offered the next year. The collaboration was an instant success resulting in award after award, and *Food & Wine* magazine named Long Shadows winery of the year in 2007.

Top: Top row, left to right: Gilles Nicault, Chester-Kidder; Ambrogio and Giovanni Folonari, Saggi; Michel Rolland, Pedestal Merlot. Middle row, left to right: John Duval, Sequel Syrah; Allen Shoup, founder; Randy Dunn, Feather Cabernet Sauvignon. Bottom row, left to right: Armin Diel, Poet's Leap; Agustin Huneeus Sr., Philippe Melka, Pirouette Red Wine.
Photograph courtesy of Long Shadows Vintners

Bottom: The Benches Vineyard is planted on a series of "benches" carved out of the earth by the Missoula floods that raced down the Columbia River during the last Ice Age.
Photograph by Andréa Johnson

Facing page: Long Shadows director of winemaking Gilles Nicault monitors a pumpover during fermentation. The wood tanks in the background are used exclusively for Pedestal Merlot at the request of Michel Rolland.
Photograph by Andréa Johnson

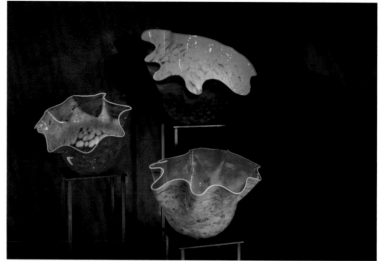

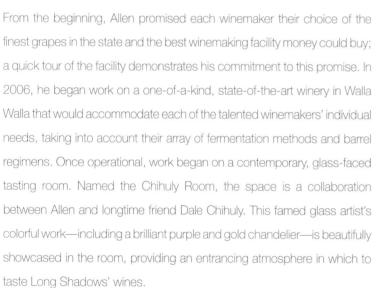

From the beginning, Allen promised each winemaker their choice of the finest grapes in the state and the best winemaking facility money could buy; a quick tour of the facility demonstrates his commitment to this promise. In 2006, he began work on a one-of-a-kind, state-of-the-art winery in Walla Walla that would accommodate each of the talented winemakers' individual needs, taking into account their array of fermentation methods and barrel regimens. Once operational, work began on a contemporary, glass-faced tasting room. Named the Chihuly Room, the space is a collaboration between Allen and longtime friend Dale Chihuly. This famed glass artist's colorful work—including a brilliant purple and gold chandelier—is beautifully showcased in the room, providing an entrancing atmosphere in which to taste Long Shadows' wines.

Of course the basis for each of the wines is fruit that knows no limits. Soon after Long Shadows was founded, Allen's priority rested on finding a long-term, keynote source for top quality grapes—and he knew just the place within Horse Heaven Hills. Formerly the Wallula Vineyard, the stunning piece

of land was purchased and renamed The Benches. Planted on the land's dramatic slope that rises nearly 1,000 feet from the banks of the Columbia River to the vineyard's peak, the vines provide nothing short of excellence. Viticultural merits abound, offering exactly the level of quality that brought Allen and his partners to the Columbia Valley in the first place.

Despite Allen's modest approach to the public and his preference to work quietly in the background while the artists, as he calls them, take center stage, it is clear that Allen and his visionary program have shaped Washington's wine industry for the better, certainly casting a long shadow that will be recognized for generations to come.

Above: A Chihuly chandelier and six of the artist's large Macchia bowls grace the Walla Walla winery's private dining and tasting room, providing a sophisticated yet comfortable, one-of-a-kind experience. A friendship between founder Allen Shoup and internationally renowned glass artist Dale Chihuly led to the winery's Chihuly Room, which houses a sensational glass art collection.

Facing page: The winery's location is a perfect complement to the surrounding landscape.

Previous pages: The acclaimed wines of Long Shadows Vintners, left to right: Sequel Syrah, Chester-Kidder New World Blend, Pedestal Merlot, Poet's Leap Riesling, Saggi Super Tuscan Blend, Pirouette Classic Bordeaux Blend, Feather Cabernet Sauvignon.
Photographs by Andréa Johnson

Poet's Leap Riesling
Pair with seared sea scallops with fennel, frisée, and red curry vinaigrette.

Chester-Kidder Red Wine
Perfect with Western Alaska king salmon with fingerling potatoes, snap peas, and truffle port jus.

Pedestal Merlot
Excellent with pan-seared duck breast with parsnip purée, green beans, and huckleberry jus.

Feather Cabernet Sauvignon
Wonderful with roasted beef tenderloin with roasted sweet onions, green beans, and blue cheese.

Tastings
By appointment only

LONG SHADOWS
DISTINGUISHED WINERIES & VINEYARDS

Mark Ryan Winery

Woodinville

Known for big, rich, and stylish red Bordeaux blends, Mark Ryan Winery began inside of a garage over a decade ago and has rapidly evolved into what *Wine & Spirits* magazine considers one of the top 100 wineries in the world. Developing a passion for wine during his low-income college years, Mark McNeilly—founder, owner, and evident namesake behind Mark Ryan Winery— worked in fine dining establishments and developed an appreciation for the heightened sensory experience that wine paired with amazing cuisine can achieve. Upon leaving school, he ventured into a wholesale wine career and had the opportunity to visit the world's top wine regions with his employer, furthering his education and fueling his interest in the industry. With an insider's advantage, Mark stopped selling wine and started buying premier grapes like syrah, grenache, mourvèdre, and viognier and converting them into highly acclaimed—and quirkily named—bottles of goodness. His first vintage, aged in his parent's garage, sold out thanks to a devoted cadre of friends and family. Since that time his small following has grown immensely, as evidenced by his title as winemaker of the year from *Seattle* magazine.

Intensely focused on eight blends, Mark and his team, which includes head winemaker Michael MacMorran and enologist Erica Orr, discerningly care for each bottle from vine to glass. Only using premium grapes from six vineyard sources on Red Mountain and Yakima Valley, one of which is the esteemed Ciel du Cheval Vineyard—the source of his sold-out first vintage—Mark places quality above all else, which explains his expedient rise.

Top and bottom: Quality grapes from vineyards on Red Mountain and Yakima Valley are the first step in making award-winning Mark Ryan Winery vintages.

Facing page: Founder, owner, and executive winemaker Mark Ryan McNeilly
Photographs by Andréa Johnson

Although the winery is located in a modest industrial space that's used for production purposes only, the tasting room is in Woodinville's whimsical Hollywood district and is open to wine lovers daily. Set up inside the Hollywood Schoolhouse, patrons can sample current vintages such as Long Haul, Dead Horse, The Dissident, and Wild Eyed Syrah—all of which have received high rankings from *Wine Spectator*, *Wine Enthusiast*, *International Wine Cellar*, and *Wine Advocate*.

The Mark Ryan tasting room is located in a space adjacent to the Hollywood Schoolhouse, a classic brick building in the heart of Woodinville's wine country. The room is eclectic in style, featuring rustic concrete floors, vintage rock-n-roll posters, and a Triumph motorcycle.

Above and left: The Mark Ryan Winery winemaking team with their families.

Facing page: Tasting wine at the Mark Ryan Winery tasting room inside the Hollywood Schoolhouse.
Photographs by Andréa Johnson

Dead Horse Cabernet Sauvignon
Pairs well with steak frites and American wagyu beef hanger steak marinated in Dead Horse wine.

Long Haul Red Blend
Excellent with roasted chicken with a lemon and rosemary pan sauce.

Wild Eyed Syrah
Spectacular with Marination Mobile's trifecta of a Spam slider with signature slaw and Nunya sauce, spicy pork taco, and miso ginger chicken taco.

The Dissident Red Blend
Superb with Seattle's Big Mario's pepperoni and sausage thin crust pizza.

Watch a video of owner Mark Ryan McNeilly and winemaker Mike MacMorran discussing the history of Mark Ryan Winery.

Maryhill Winery

Goldendale

Since opening its doors, Maryhill Winery has won close to 1,000 awards in both national and international competitions, making it no wonder that out of 700 wineries *Wine Press Northwest* named it Washington Winery of the Year. Winemaker Richard Batchelor produces 80,000 cases of wine each year using 24 varietals from surrounding vineyards in the Columbia Valley. The New Zealand native claims a personal affection for estate cabernet sauvignon while the property specialties include zinfandel and viognier. Although the 28 wines created at Maryhill contribute to the winery's reputation, it is the unparalleled views that merit it as a top destination.

Perched atop a bluff overlooking the world-renowned Columbia Gorge, Maryhill Winery was incorporated in 1999 and opened to the public in 2001. Originally from Spokane, Washington, owners Craig and Vicki Leuthold experimented in the wine industry for more than two decades before founding Maryhill. Beginning in an enological society, the couple became attracted to viticulture and winery operations and eventually partnered in a starter winery to get a hands-on feel for the ins and outs of the industry. Inspired by the experience, they acquired land in a legendary area on the southernmost tip of the Columbia Valley called Maryhill.

Derived from influential businessman Samuel Hill, the region's namesake honors his wife Mary and the couple's history in Washington. An instrumental figure in Washington's development, Sam's interests in road construction and law, among other things, led him to purchase 5,300 acres of land in 1907 with the intention of building an independent farming community named after his wife. Unfortunately his dream dissolved in 1917, but the Hill family mansion lives on as the Maryhill Museum, just west of the winery.

Top and facing page: Winemaker Richard Batchelor, a New Zealand native, stands amongst the Hanging Bench zinfandel to the east of the winery. In the distance, more zinfandel and moscato proliferate near Indian Rock. The climate in which Maryhill Winery resides provides ideal growing conditions for its 24 different varietals.
Photographs by Andréa Johnson

Bottom: The sun streams in through the west window of Maryhill's 3,000-square-foot tasting room, which welcomes 75,000 visitors each year.
Photograph by Richard Hallman

Reminiscent of a Tuscan villa, the winery's tiled roof and stucco finish complement the surrounding countryside. Inside, the 3,000-square-foot gift shop and tasting room charms guests with an impressive 20-foot-long Brunswick bar, made of quartersawn tiger oak from the late 1800s. Its bold presence and intricate carvings demand attention, along with a huge selection of fun merchandise.

A beautiful terrace with a vine-covered arbor and picnic areas offers the perfect setting to sit, sip, marvel at the views, and enjoy live music every weekend during summer months. Guests are also welcome to play ball on the four world-class bocce courts, just a short walk away. A commanding 4,000-seat amphitheater hosts a summertime concert series, featuring artists such as Bob Dylan, Jackson Brown, and the Counting Crows, and offers magnificent views of the gorge below.

Top: A 100-year-old Brunswick bar proudly stands as the focal point of the 3,000-square-foot tasting room. Owners Craig and Vicki Leuthold are pictured with winery mascot Mr. Potter, their Great Pyrenees.
Photograph by Jackie Johnston, www.winecountrycreations.com

Bottom: Some of the more than 1,000 awards earned by Maryhill Winery are displayed on the Brunswick bar in the tasting room. Accolades include being named the Washington winery of the year and best destination winery.
Photograph by Joe Garoutte

Facing page: Winemaker Richard Batchelor surveys some viognier from a precarious perch atop the macro bins. Each bin holds approximately 800 pounds of the 800 to 1,000 tons of handpicked grapes Maryhill Winery receives every year.
Photograph by Andrêa Johnson

Working at a modern-day Shangri-La comes with certain expectations. For several years now, winemaker Richard Batchelor has continually exceeded them, earning more awards and accolades with each new wine released. Prior to joining Maryhill, Richard's work in California received high marks from local sources and also on the world stage. Capturing the attention of publications such as *Wine Spectator* with numerous 90-plus point vintages have made his wines recognizable and highly sought-after. In addition to previous experience as an enologist in New Zealand, Richard holds a postgraduate degree in viticulture and enology from Lincoln University in Christchurch. He is responsible for directing all production activities at the winery, including harvest coordination, winemaking, and bottling beloved vintages like Proprietors Reserve Cabernet Sauvignon and Reserve Grenache, Craig and Vicki's personal favorites.

With an estate this large, a faithful four-legged friend and watchdog is a must-have. Craig and Vicki's 130-pound Great Pyrenees named Mr. Potter greets guests with a wag, representing the joy that both Craig and Vicki feel for every patron that comes to share in the beauty and bounty of the winery. Whether by taste, sound, or by sight, a visit to Maryhill satisfies the senses perfectly.

Top: Access to four world-class bocce courts are complimentary for all winery visitors. A picnic area and large lawn make for a great family gathering or leisurely afternoon watching the fun.
Photograph by Joe Garoutte

Middle: The arbor-covered terrace welcomes guests year-round. Live music is available from Memorial Day through Labor Day as guests overlook the vistas of the Columbia River Gorge.
Photograph by Joe Garoutte

Bottom: Maryhill Winery has hosted concerts in its natural amphitheater since 2003. With the completion of the new permanent stage in 2008, the winery offers a world-class listening experience for approximately 4,000 guests per show.
Photograph by Joe Garoutte

Facing page: Winemaker Richard Batchelor enjoys one of the winery's 200-plus growing days while overlooking the Sandhill zinfandel and muscato di canelli near Indian Rock, east of the tasting room.
Photograph by Andréa Johnson

VINE & FARE

Reserve Cabernet Sauvignon
Pair with a boneless barbecued leg of lamb stuffed with brown rice, nuts, and dried fruit.

Viognier
Pair with spicy Dungeness crab casserole with mandolin-shaved salad.

Reserve Zinfandel
Pair with homemade Reserve Zinfandel spaghetti sauce using fresh tomatoes, garlic, onions, peppers, and seasonings and poured over a pasta of choice.

Tastings
Open to the public daily, year-round

Matthews

Woodinville

I n the early 1990s, Matthews was one of the first boutique wineries to open in Woodinville, quickly earning a reputation for its high-quality cabernet sauvignon and Bordeaux-style blends. Sauvignon blanc and syrah were soon added to its yearly lineup. Over the years, the winery has received much recognition from both the public and wine worlds alike, including high marks and awards from *Wine Spectator*, and Robert Parker's *Wine Advocate*. Today the winery's flagship wine is the Columbia Valley Claret. Notably, Matthews is one of only 17 wineries in the country that is able to use this restricted, trademarked term for a Bordeaux-style red wine.

Located in the heart of the Woodinville wine country, now home to more than 70 other wineries and tasting rooms, Matthews sits on eight acres overlooking the peaceful Woodinville Valley and houses both a tasting room and the Matthews Estate House, which is a wonderful location for special events, weddings, and overnight accommodations.

Winemaker Aryn Morell, who spent his childhood in Washington, returned after a five-year stint in Napa Valley where he worked for wineries such as Golden State Vintners, Edgewood Estates, and Silver Oak. Aryn's innovative application of proven California vinification techniques to high-quality Washington fruit is producing some remarkable wines.

The winery is under the direction of a local family who enjoys running the day-to-day operations. The Cellar Building, which houses the tasting room and barrel room, is the site for a number of exciting events every month, from classes to live music. No matter what time of year, a good time and great wine can always be found at Matthews.

Top: A hot air balloon ride over Matthews on a warm summer day.
Photograph by Andréa Johnson

Middle: Live music every Friday evening at the winery.
Photograph by Andréa Johnson

Bottom: Owners, the Otis family.
Photograph by Keith Megay

Facing page: The vista deck overlooking peaceful Woodinville Valley in the heart of Woodinville wine country.
Photograph by Andréa Johnson

Mercer Estates Winery

Prosser

The Mercer family has been living and farming in Prosser for more than 125 years, the Hogue family for more than 70. When the two families—each wine pioneers in their own right—decided to join together in 2006, they created Mercer Estates Winery, a winery known not only for its beautiful merlot and fresh, delicious riesling, but also for its astonishing soil and climate diversity. The winery's achievements can also be attributed to the knowledge, history, and passion that each family brings to the partnership—intangible yet vital ingredients for success.

The variety in terroir comes from the contributions of the two family AVAs: the Hogue/Harle family vineyards bring the Yakima Valley AVA, and the Mercer family vineyards offer the Horse Heaven Hills AVA. The warmer Horse Heaven Hills is known for producing some of the best red grapes in Washington State, which in turn produces wines of great body, structure, and complexity. The cooler Yakima Valley is known for its riesling, chardonnay, sauvignon blanc, and pinot gris, white wines with balanced acidity and beautiful flavor profiles. There is also an estate vineyard on the Columbia River called Spice Cabinet, which produces gorgeous wines from more exotic varieties such as sangiovese, malbec, grenache, and petit verdot.

Owners Rob and Brenda Mercer, Ron and Barb Harle, and Mike and Dora Hogue are continuing on with a tradition that most still marvel at: two families who could have been rivals deciding instead to partner up and produce premium Washington wines together. When Mike Hogue sold his respected winery The Hogue Cellars in 2001, he waited five years for the non-compete clause to expire before taking the advice of Barb and Ron and teaming with

Top: The owners of Mercer Estates Winery (clockwise from left): Barb and Ron Harle, Rob and Brenda Mercer, Mike and Dora Hogue.

Bottom: A cluster of grapes before being turned into Mercer Estates wine.

Facing page: Looking south over Spice Cabinet Vineyard in the Horse Heaven Hills.
Photographs by Andréa Johnson

their old family friends, the Mercers. Winemaker David Forsyth and cellar master Dave Copeland, who have spent more than 30 years making wine together in Washington State, came along with Mike. A production facility was built in 2007, with the barrel room following a year later and the tasting room opening the year after that.

Architecture that is simple, agricultural, extremely functional, and environmentally conscious marks the winery. Some of its lauded conservation efforts include energy and water conservation, integrated pest management, soil protection, and wildlife habitat improvement. As a result of Mercer Estates' sustainable practices, the winery and its estate vineyards have drastically reduced power consumption, and water consumption has been reduced by nearly half of the industry average per gallon of wine.

A tasting bar to sample some of the wines that have received numerous local, regional, national, and international awards over the years is available, but a relaxing, sit-down experience is more what the owners prefer. Photographs detailing the histories of both families line the walls,

and visitors are able to tour the entire facility—no area is off-limits—while learning about Washington wine country.

Besides educating visitors, Mercer Estates gives back to its community with seasonal celebrations designed to honor and recognize those who donate to local charities. The summer barbecue, held in late July, is a down-home party with dancing, music, s'mores bar, and plenty of wine. The winter Wine and Dine is an elegant, candle-lit dinner in January. While certainly a good time, these events are only the beginning of Mercer Estates' charitable nature. Both owners and employees are proud to participate in A Night Out in Prosser, benefiting the local hospital, and the Auction of Washington Wines held at Chateau Ste. Michelle, an event that has raised millions for Seattle Children's Hospital.

Above left: Ryan and Ron Harle and T.J. and Rob Mercer overlook tanks in winery's the production facility.

Top: Hospitality manager Jenna Hannan displays the Mercer Estates line-up.

Bottom: Overlooking Spice Cabinet Vineyard in "Greenie," Bud Mercer's 1956 International pickup.

Facing page: The Hogue, Mercer, and Harle families on the Mercer Estates Winery grounds.

Previous pages: Ron Harle stands at a crossroads in Zephyr Ridge Estate Vineyard, with the Columbia River in the distance.
Photographs by Andréa Johnson

Mercer Estates Riesling
Pair with ginger crème brûlée with honey and nectarines.

Mercer Sauvignon Blanc
Pair with goat cheese with olives, lemon, and thyme on crisp rosemary flatbread.

Mercer Cabernet Sauvignon
Pair with mustard- and herb-crusted rack of lamb.

Mercer Petit Verdot
Pair with Latin skirt steak topped with avocados, jalapeños, tomatoes, and cilantro.

Tastings
Open to the public Wednesday through Sunday, March through December, and by appointment

Watch a video of Rob Mercer explaining the history of Mercer Estates Winery, and find out what you can only sample at the on-site tasting room.

Milbrandt Vineyards

Prosser

A stately building, much like a Tuscan villa with elegant stone accents and charming courtyards, sits atop a grassy green slope in Prosser, a small town near the Yakima River. The beautiful habitat serves as the home of Milbrandt Vineyards, owned by brothers Butch and Jerry Milbrandt. The vineyard operation, founded in 1997, is comprised of 12 estate sites totaling 2,000 acres. Milbrandt Vineyards has earned an enviable reputation around the country for varietals that expound upon both Washington State's and Milbrandt Vineyards' ability to cultivate wines to their fullest potential.

What initially began as a family-learned farming business escalated over the years to become the sophisticated palette of Milbrandt Vineyards wines. Both Butch and Jerry spent nearly three decades farming row crops and apples since they became farming partners in 1969. After 28 years, they began focusing on a new crop that was quickly growing in demand: wine grapes. At that time, viticultural expert James McFerran joined the team to assist with the planting of the vines, a particular and crucial science to ensure that the correct grape varieties were grown in the right climates and sites.

Their vineyards became so renowned that they were encouraged to establish the Milbrandt Vineyards winery in 2005 and began producing their own wines under the Milbrandt Vineyards label. With an acute knowledge of the terroir of each of their vineyards, Butch and Jerry focus on avoiding over-manipulation of the wines while building on the vineyards' strengths to produce fully ripe, fruit-driven flavors. The vines are primarily located in the Wahluke Slope AVA, with the exception of the Evergreen and Ancient Lakes vineyards in the town of Quincy, where the Milbrandts grew up. Among their 27 varieties, the Traditions Riesling is a strong favorite for both wine enthusiasts and visiting guests alike. Grown in their Evergreen

Top: Syrah grapes in Clifton Vineyards in the vérasion stage.

Bottom: Milbrandt Vineyards' Rhône-style blend of syrah, mourvèdre, grenache, and viognier.

Facing page: Clifton Bluff Vineyard overlooks the Columbia River in the Wahluke Slope AVA.
Photographs by Mark Roberts Photography

Vineyard, the Milbrandt's riesling reveals aromatic notes of ripe apricots, Elberta peaches, honey, tangerine, and orange blossoms.

The brothers' vineyards produce 40,000 cases of wine each year, which are distributed in 48 states. Their 2009 The Estates Cabernet Sauvignon beat out the California entries to win the coveted Best of Class award at the 2012 San Francisco Chronicle Wine Competition, and their viognier won a Double Gold medal—not bad for a Washington winery entered in a California wine competition. *Food & Wine* magazine also crowned them a winner of the 2011 F&W American Wine Awards and named them one of the five most thrilling new producers in America. Monthly wine dinners and regular tasting and special events beckon guests new and old to the vineyards on a regular basis, as the Milbrandt Vineyards tasting room is open daily, year-round. And with family ownership set to continue—Butch's son, Buckley, and Jerry's daughter, Kelly, are both Northwest wine representatives for the company—Milbrandt Vineyards is sure to age as well as a fine wine.

Top and facing page: The welcoming tasting room at Milbrandt Vineyards.

Middle: Butch and Jerry in their favorite location: a field of vines.

Bottom: The Estates Grenache and Viognier, two award-winning varietals.
Photographs by Mark Roberts Photography

Traditions Riesling
Delectable with pan-seared jumbo sea scallops or Asian fusion entrées.

The Estates Malbec
A tasteful companion for filet mignon Oscar or beef brisket.

The Estates Cabernet Sauvignon
Delicious with rack of lamb.

Sentinel
Best paired with beef bourguignon.

Tastings
Open to the public daily, year-round

Nefarious Cellars

Chelan

When it's time for owners Heather and Dean Neff to critique each other's wines at Nefarious Cellars, brutal honesty is the name of the game, leaving some to think the husband-and-wife duo is a bit crazy. Why would any spouse in his or her right mind think it's a good idea to candidly assess a mate's labor of love? Yet that's exactly what the Neffs do, and really what makes them succeed.

Crafting wine together has always been Heather and Dean's dream. They began in 1998, planting a test block vineyard of numerous varietals in the Methow Valley near Lake Chelan. Feeling drawn to Oregon, they moved to the Willamette Valley to work with pinot noir, but found themselves back in Washington in 2004 to pursue the state's bountiful winemaking possibilities. The couple established Nefarious Cellars on the south shore of Lake Chelan— still the only winery with a tasting bar facing the lake—and planted a few vineyards in the area. Near the original test block in the Columbia Valley AVA, they planted Rocky Mother Vineyard with syrah and Stone's Throw Vineyard with riesling, both appropriately named for the land's makeup. At the winery, they planted Defiance Vineyard with syrah, viognier, and malbec, resisting popular opinion that the area was too cool to ripen red grapes. They also began sourcing a few other varietals, including cabernet sauvignon, cabernet franc, grenache, sauvignon blanc, and aligoté, from other vineyards.

In all aspects, from viticulture to winemaking, Heather and Dean embrace the idea that the least amount of intervention will craft the best wines, allowing the fruit to speak for itself. They liken it to cooking, where there's nothing better than slicing into a beautiful, fresh tomato or taking a bite out of a plump, juicy peach. Starting with this common concept, Heather and Dean then branch off into their own avenues: Heather crafts white wines and Dean the reds.

Top: The winemaking facility at Nefarious Cellars.

Bottom: Winemakers and owners Dean and Heather Neff.

Facing page: Defiance Vineyard at Nefarious Cellars in Lake Chelan.
Photographs by Patrick Bennett

Not only does this allow each to inject their own personality and style into the wines, making them more distinct, but this separation also allows them to honestly critique each other's creations without the emotional investment that builds as the winemaker lovingly crafts the wine.

Seeing this complementary relationship firsthand and tasting its rewards is quite something. Easy to find, the winery is Lake Chelan's red barn on the hill. Inside, the minimalist tasting room is all about the wine and the beautiful view. Heather and Dean impart a casual atmosphere, ready to share their passion by answering questions, serving the tasting flight of four wines, and giving a tour of their operations. And while nefarious actually means wicked, it's more accurate to define Nefarious Cellars as wickedly amazing, both in taste and experience.

Above: Efrain Rangel works his magic on the crusher/destemmer.

Left: Cellar master Anton Mayer sorts syrah as it comes across the shaker table.

Facing page: Dean, George, Heather, and Cooper Neff have a little fun at the winery.
Photographs by Patrick Bennett

Nefarious Cellars Defiance Vineyard Viognier
Excellent with scallops or crab.

Nefarious Cellars Stone's Throw Riesling
Pair with Asian or Indian cuisine.

Nefarious Cellars Defiance Vineyard Syrah
Delicious with braised beef or grilled pork tenderloin.

Nefarious Cellars Defiance Vineyard Malbec
Luscious with grilled prawns or sausage with spicy barbecue sauce.

Tastings
Open to the public, seasonally

Watch a video of Dean and Heather Neff explaining why
their wickedly good wines live up to their namesake.

Nefarious
CELLARS

2009
ESTATE SYRAH
ROCKY MOTHER VINEYARD
ALCOHOL 14.8% BY VOLUME

Northstar Winery

Walla Walla

Just as the North Star has been used for centuries as a directional guide for mariners, Northstar Winery was established in 1992 to create world-class merlot-based wines, guiding wine aficionados and novice drinkers alike to recognize all that Washington has to offer—including merlots that rival the best in the world.

While the state enjoys the same latitude as France's Bordeaux region, it boasts the added benefit of a longer season for ripening, which is the perfect environment for fruit that results in full-bodied, vivid merlot. Founded with the goal of creating Washington's best merlot wines, Northstar sources fruit from the top vineyard sites in the state for its Columbia Valley and Walla Walla Valley merlots.

Forming the backbone of Northstar wines, merlot fruit is enhanced to add texture and complexity by carefully blending in other traditional Bordeaux varietals, a "spice rack" of components according to winemaker David "Merf" Merfeld. He relies on cabernet sauvignon to soften with bright cherry and raspberry flavors, petit verdot for color and structure, and cabernet franc to layer in an olive herbal tone.

The final offerings include a Walla Walla merlot, Columbia Valley merlot, Stella Maris red blend, and a Stella Blanca house white wine sémillon only available in Northstar's tasting room. But these blends aren't something just anyone can achieve.

Top: Northstar's estate vineyard in Walla Walla.

Bottom: Northstar winemaker David "Merf" Merfeld measures tannin levels in the winery's state-of-the-art lab.

Facing page: Overlooking the Blue Mountains, Northstar's patio is a popular destination for visitors to the Walla Walla Valley.
Photographs by Andrèa Johnson

Requiring equal parts winemaking expertise and artistry—qualities which Merf can certainly be said to possess—the process includes tailoring the barrel regimen for each vineyard lot to fit that vineyard's character and history. His knowledge of the vineyards is virtually unmatched, as he constantly evaluates the lots to create the perfect balance of varietal purity, fruit intensity, and harmonious tannins. After bottling, the wines enjoy an aging process of up to 18 months to ensure that first sip is delicious whether the bottle is opened immediately or in 20 years.

All of this happens at Northstar's state-of-the-art winery in Walla Walla, where lush vines and the gorgeous backdrop of the Blue Mountains look like a postcard from a stunning vacation. Amid this breathtaking setting, though, passionate activities are taking place, from the careful creation of the top-tier wines to the cutting-edge lab where the winemaking team performs tannin management research to benefit the industry.

A perfect example of Northstar's commitment to moving merlot forward, a 2012 release made from 100 percent merlot utilizes the most innovative techniques and technology to create a merlot comparable to the best in the world. Whether visitors' interests include touring the top-notch facility, tasting the acclaimed wines, or learning about Washington merlots, the experience will not disappoint. In fact, it will lead to a deeper appreciation for the state's unbelievable fruit and wine.

Top: Winemaker Merf works in the cellar at Northstar.
Photograph by Kevin Cruff

Bottom: Visitors to Northstar can taste through the winery's portfolio of merlots and component wines.
Photograph by Andréa Johnson

Facing page: Located just south of downtown Walla Walla, Northstar is open to visitors seven days a week.
Photograph by Andréa Johnson

Northstar Columbia Valley Merlot
Divine with roasted leg of lamb with herbs.

Northstar Walla Walla Merlot
Tantalizing with grilled ribeye with blue cheese.

Stella Maris
Appetizing with a juicy grilled burger and seasoned sweet potato fries.

Tastings
Open to the public daily

NORTHSTAR

Obelisco Estate
Red Mountain

Obelisks, which to this day still serve as powerful symbols, were first carved and raised as early as 2000 BC by Egyptians who quarried the large, pyramid-capped monuments out of single, solid pieces of granite that were then inscribed with praises to the gods and the name of the pharaoh. Only exceptional craftsmen took part in the carving process, leaving permanent evidence of the civilization and the specific generation.

Upon Doug Long's founding of Obelisco Estate in 2004, the name was selected to symbolize the connection to ancient obelisks, which represent their creators' mark on the earth. And just as the four-sided monuments were carved out of the earth, Obelisco's wine is carved out of Red Mountain terroir.

Born out of Doug's passion for wine and his history of viticultural success—he and his two brothers owned a Napa Valley vineyard and winery that continues to receive high marks from many prestigious publications and organizations—Obelisco Estate is a small, 30-acre vineyard located on the southwest slope of Red Mountain, designed to produce intensely complex, rich red wines.

A firm believer that world-class wines require world-class fruit, Doug's philosophy is designed around producing great fruit. With the vineyard's original planting in 2004, Doug was a pioneer in Washington through encouraging lower yields per plant by spacing the vines close together—about 2,000 vines an acre compared to the average 800 vines per acre at that time. Combined with cluster management to keep production down to four pounds per plant, the resulting fruit is intensely concentrated for outstanding quality.

Top: Doug Long walks the vineyard and tastes the fruit before every harvest.
Photograph by Ken Abbott, Obelisco Estate

Bottom: An inviting glass of Obelisco Estate's Electrum Cabernet.
Photograph by Ken Abbott, Obelisco Estate

Facing page: Harvest time at Obelisco, with the small berry fruit that is the vineyard's hallmark.
Photograph by Doug Long, Obelisco Estate

The estate's flagship wine, an upper-end cabernet called Electrum, is crafted from a blend of 90 percent cabernet, 2.5 percent malbec, and 7.5 percent merlot, which represents the exact proportions of the vineyard's fruit and is exactly what Doug envisions when he considers Red Mountain.

All of Obelisco Estate's wines are noted for structure, acidity, and intense varietal character, and every vintage has received 90-plus points—an incredible accomplishment. In fact, the experience is all about tasting good fruit, directly relating to Doug's focus on the vineyard's quality. Every sip is a savory taste of the fruity, berry quality of wine that is never masked by heavy tannins or over oak. It's all about elegance in wine production that doesn't overwhelm but leaves an impressive mark that will be remembered for generations, just as the ancient obelisks were.

Top: The Vilar and Patterson families represent the third and fourth generations of grape growing and winemaking.
Photograph by Sara Harris

Bottom: Doug Long resting against the winery door at the end of the 2012 harvest.
Photograph by Andréa Johnson

Facing page: Obelisco a day before harvest begins.
Photograph by Ken Abbott, Obelisco Estate

Estate Cabernet
Perfect with all red meats, especially with a maple- and apple-flavored dinner sausage.

Estate Merlot
Wonderful with gravy dishes like beef bourguignon.

Estate Malbec
Great for lamb as well as pork dishes.

Electrum Cabernet
Enjoyable with everything from steak to dark chocolate.

Tastings
Open to the public Saturdays and Sundays or by appointment

Page Cellars

Woodinville

Not many people would find a direct link between aviation and winemaking; at first glance, they appear to have nothing in common. But Jim Page has seen the connection between the two evolve greatly since he and his wife, Rothelle, founded Page Cellars in 2000.

As a corporate pilot, Jim has the opportunity to see the world, transporting his often high-profile passengers to destinations many only dream of. On several occasions, he was invited to tour various high-end wineries in California and Washington along with his passengers. His exposure to the wineries piqued his interest in the possibility of crafting his own wine and soon he began making that dream a reality.

After working with a consulting winemaker to learn the process and develop his palate—which he explains that he did in reverse because he had to find wines that were flawed to identify those components—Jim and Rothelle founded the winery at the start of the new millennium. Jim continued his flying career, assuming the hands-on tasks as his flight schedule allowed and relying heavily on Rothelle, who Jim identifies as the "glue that has held the winery together."

The result of the Pages' dream, which is founded on a passion for making the best wine possible from each vintage, is premium wines and provincial prices. Using fruit from the finest vineyards in Washington State, Jim and Rothelle ardently follow one concept: to let it be. They believe that minimal intervention in the winemaking process allows the fruit to express itself, showing distinctive characteristics that are only available from that vineyard's

Top: Rothelle and Jim Page, otherwise known as "the boss" and "the help."
Photograph by Patrick Bennett

Bottom: Corkage for one.
Photograph by Patrick Bennett

Facing page: Page Cellars' techniques and respect for natural balance allows the rhythm of the vineyard and the creativity of the winemaker to enter into a convenient conversation.
Photograph courtesy of Page Cellars

specific location, microclimate, and soil. Jim has also discovered his purist tendencies; he prefers to produce wines of a single varietal with little or no blending. His techniques and respect for natural balance allow the rhythm of the vineyard and his own creativity to craft premium small-lot red and white wines, including reds like the Preface Cabernet and the infamous Lick My Lips Syrah.

So what has Jim seen that connects aviation and winemaking, other than the fact that one led to the other in his life? He explains that Mother Nature plays a large role in each of his careers, often shaping and dictating the path that must be taken. He has also noticed that both appeal to his love of the hands-on process, where the success is solely his responsibility and he is in control of the future result. Quite a responsibility, many would say, but Jim and Rothelle gladly take it on, relying on friends and family who continue to help them offer fine wines over which they can live, laugh, and love.

Left: Jim's "other office" may be 37,000 feet in the air, but working in the winery helps keep him grounded.
Top and middle photographs courtesy of Page Cellars
Bottom photograph by Patrick Bennett

Facing page: Lick My Lips Syrah is just the beginning of Page Cellars' impressive portfolio of wines.
Photograph by Patrick Bennett

Libra Winemaker's Blend
Pair with grilled pork tenderloin and fingerling potato and apple salad with hazelnuts, radicchio, and a mustard vinaigrette.

Preface Cabernet Sauvignon
Amazing with juniper-crusted venison rack atop mashed sweet potatoes and pancetta-sautéed brussel sprouts, all topped with huckleberry jus.

Autumn Chase Viognier
Delectable with Dungeness crab salad featuring Belgian endive, celeriac, grapefruit, and tarragon and celery leaf.

Sentimental Blonde Sauvignon Blanc
Incredible with black cod atop roasted parsnip purée and savoy cabbage, garnished with Washington black truffle slices.

Tastings
Open to the public Saturday and Sunday

Pepper Bridge Winery

Walla Walla

F ounded in 1989 on 40 acres of land in Walla Walla's undiscovered wine country, Pepper Bridge Vineyard was initially planted wholly in merlot and later in cabernet sauvignon. Over three decades, these and other Bordeaux varietals have grown to inhabit over 400 acres between two estate vineyards, which is where Pepper Bridge Winery obtains all fruit used in making 100 percent estate vineyard, Walla Walla Valley, certified-sustainably farmed wines.

To say that Norm McKibben is a driven man is an understatement. Largely responsible for the start of Walla Walla's flourishing wine industry, Norm is referred to by friends as "Stormin' Norman" due to his pioneering spirit and can-do attitude. While searching for his post-retirement piece of paradise, Norm, a career engineer, discovered a lovely plot of land where he could grow old while growing apples. The land was once a farm belonging to the Pepper family and served as a land bridge for travelers passing over the Walla Walla River by stagecoach, which became the area's name and the winery's namesake.

Ray Goff joined as winery partner in 1998 after working for Anheuser-Busch as vice president of corporate purchasing, and president of its agricultural subsidiaries. During a business trip to Washington, Ray turned his attention from hops to grapes at a winery in Prosser, where he acknowledged the singular flavor of Washington's rare terroir and was quickly converted. Something of a wine aficionado himself, Ray ended annual visits to Napa's wine country and turned his attention to helping the Walla Walla Valley establish itself as one of the premier wine regions in the nation.

Top: The Pepper Bridge Winery tasting room entrance.

Bottom: Pepper Bridge Winery managing partner Norm McKibben and his son, Eric, part of the winery's second generation.

Facing page: The gravity-flow production tiers of Pepper Bridge Winery, nestled among its estate vineyards with the Blue Mountains in the background
Photographs by Andréa Johnson

The third founding partner and excellent palate behind Pepper Bridge vintages is the winemaker, Jean-François Pellet. Degreed in both viticulture and winemaking from his native country of Switzerland, Jean-François came to Pepper Bridge with decades of experience, springing from his childhood passion and father's profession of making wine. After working for wineries in Switzerland, Spain, and California, he was drawn to Walla Walla by the alluring estate vineyards as well as the opportunity to co-design and implement a gravity-flow winery. Since arriving in Walla Walla in 1999, Jean-François has served as lead winemaker and has also established several new vineyards in the valley. He also founded and currently serves as the vice president of VINEA, an organization committed to sustainable agriculture in the Walla Walla Valley.

Son Eric McKibben and daughter Travis Goff have since joined the winery as partners and currently work with Norm, Ray, and Jean-François to produce some of Walla Walla's most celebrated vintages.

Top: Pepper Bridge Winery partners Ray Goff and his daughter, Travis Goff.

Bottom: Pepper Bridge Winery partner and winemaker Jean-François Pellet.

Facing page: Pepper Bridge Winery's tasting room, surrounded by one of its estate vineyards.
Photographs by Andréa Johnson

Cabernet Sauvignon
Taste with braised beef chuck roast and grilled asparagus.

Merlot
Pair with tender bison ribeye with morel mushrooms and shallots in a merlot reduction.

Trine
Sip with grilled elk tenderloin with huckleberry reduction next to roasted red potatoes.

Tastings
Open daily, year-round
Also available at Woodinville tasting room

Watch a video of owners Ray Goff and Norm McKibben, along with winemaker Jean-François Pellet, discussing their perspectives on winemaking.

PEPPER BRIDGE WINERY · PB · WALLA WALLA VALLEY

Quilceda Creek Vintners

Snohomish

By all accounts, Quilceda Creek Vintners has perfected the art of doing one thing and doing it well. With a dedicated focus, Quilceda's founders Alex and Jeannette Golitzin have created a winery solely around unbelievable cabernet sauvignon. From their first commercial release in 1979—when the winery had just been established as the 12th bonded winery in Washington—to more recent releases that have received numerous perfect 100-point ratings from Robert Parker's *Wine Advocate,* every vintage consistently proves the excellence of Washington fruit and the talent of the Quilceda team, causing collectors around the world to seek out the wine.

Alex's introduction to winemaking began early. With a family heritage that includes Prince Lev Sergeievich Golitzin, acclaimed winemaker to Russian Tsar Nicholas II, winemaking was in his veins. But what really inspired Alex was living in San Francisco as a youth and spending time with his uncle André Tchelistcheff, the legendary winemaker at Napa Valley's Beaulieu Vineyards and a founding father of the modern California wine industry. Over the years his passion for wine continued to grow, and by the time Alex and wife Jeannette moved to Washington for Alex's career as a chemical engineer, his obsession for winemaking was at a fever pitch. So in 1978, Alex and Jeannette founded Quilceda Creek Vintners to focus on creating the ultimate cabernet sauvignon, ignoring those skeptical of Washington's then-unfounded realm of fine red wine.

Top: Old-vine cabernet sauvignon from Champoux Vineyard in the Horse Heaven Hills is one of the primary sources for Quilceda Creek's flagship wine.

Bottom: Paul Golitzin (left) and his father Alex share winemaking responsibilities at Quilceda Creek. Together, the two have proven to be a prodigious force in the wine world.

Facing page: Quilceda Creek has built an international reputation for its world-class cabernet sauvignon.
Photographs by Andréa Johnson

Son Paul Golitzin assumed winemaking responsibilities with his father in 1992. With a commitment to quality that rivaled his parents', Paul focused the winery's attention on its greatest asset: the vineyards of the Columbia Valley. As a result, Quilceda Creek selectively acquired a handful of vineyards over the next decade, a move that catapulted the wines to a new level of excellence. In addition to partnership with Paul Champoux of Champoux Vineyard, the Golitzin family also developed the Galitzine Vineyard with Ciel du Cheval's Jim Holmes, as well as the Palengat Vineyard in the Horse Heaven Hills.

The winery itself is a state-of-the-art facility that appropriately mirrors the quality of the wine. It is closed to the public except for one weekend a year when private mailing list members gather at the winery to pick up their allotment and celebrate the release. But what goes on behind those closed doors is no mystery. Wine connoisseurs and novices alike agree that Quilceda's cabernet sauvignons display dense fruit flavors, smooth tannins, and wonderful balance, rivaling any in the world.

Above left: Collectors from around the U.S. travel to Quilceda Creek for a rare glimpse inside the winery when the Golitzins open their doors to private mailing list guests in the spring.
Photograph by Andréa Johnson

Top: The team at Quilceda Creek is known for creating exceptional cabernet, vintage after vintage.
Photograph by Andréa Johnson

Bottom: With a single-minded focus on cabernet sauvignon since its first vintage in 1979, Quilceda Creek has become one of the most storied wineries in the country.
Photograph by Mark Bauschke

Facing page: Planted in 2001, Galitzine Vineyard is located on Red Mountain and is a joint venture between Quilceda Creek and Jim Holmes of Red Mountain's famed Ciel du Cheval.
Photograph by Andréa Johnson

Cabernet Sauvingon Columbia Valley
Pair with duck breast with red wine reduction.

Galitzine Vineyard Cabernet Sauvignon
Pair with herb-grilled rack of lamb with mustard sauce.

Palengat Red Wine
Pair with grilled pork tenderloin with port and dried cranberry sauce.

Columbia Valley Red Wine
Pair with chicken breast in cambozola and morel cream sauce
with port reduction.

Tastings
Closed to the public

Reininger Winery
Walla Walla

Established in 1997, Reininger Winery is well known for its dedication to bringing out the best in Walla Walla fruit and showcasing the true character of the Walla Walla Valley. Guided by founder, winemaker, and outdoorsman Chuck Reininger, the winery produces an array of classic, finely structured wines that reflect both the family's personalities and an ongoing commitment to retain the highest quality, care, and consistency in winemaking. For Chuck, making wine has become a way to harness his passion for nature, adventure, and his love of the great outdoors into a product that can be shared with the community.

After working at a local winery in the early 1990s and dabbling with home winemaking, Chuck finally pursued his dream of opening a winery. He and wife Tracy—née Tucker—a fifth-generation Walla Walla native, first set up shop in an old Army Air Corps crash house, fondly nicknamed the "Shack-teau," where they focused on limited production, terroir-inspired red wines. With the addition of Tucker family members Jay and Cyndi, Kelly and Ann, and Terry and Ronnie in 2003, the winery relocated to seven acres just west of Walla Walla, where it now operates in a beautifully renovated winery and tasting room.

Throughout Reininger's evolution, it has retained its commitment to the Walla Walla community and its fondness for the valley. For the Reininger and Tucker families, winemaking is all about experiencing the journey and ascending to the top. Reininger winery has twice been named the winery of the year under the Artisan Winery of the Year category by *Wine & Spirits* magazine.

Top: Winemaker and founder Chuck Reininger.
Photograph by Colby D. Kuschatka

Middle: The Reininger tasting room, which was built from reclaimed potato shed wood, features a bar countertop made of Walla Walla basalt and Reininger vineyard vines woven between the barrel staves on the bar front.
Photograph by Andréa Johnson

Bottom: Barrel tasting.
Photograph by Andréa Johnson

Facing page: Reininger Winery's entrance.
Photograph by Colby D. Kuschatka

Ross Andrew Winery

Walla Walla

A Seattle-area native, Ross Andrew Mickel's path to wine production began on a 2006 fly-fishing trip with Canlis Restaurant heir Mark Canlis. It was during this afternoon on the river that Mark asked Ross if he had any interest in learning about wine from the restaurant perspective; Ross jumped at the opportunity to learn from one of the most impressive restaurants in the U.S. While working under Canlis' master sommelier Rob Bigelow, Ross realized that wine was going to be his life's journey.

It was from here that he launched into traveling the globe—Australia, South America, Europe, and South Africa—to learn all he could about food and wine. Upon returning home and realizing it was time to get something going, he landed a harvest job as a cellar rat at the iconic Washington State winery DeLille Cellars. This was immediately followed by a vintage at one of Australia's leading wineries, Rosemount Estate. Returning to the U.S., Ross was hired by arguably one of Washington's most highly respected producers, Betz Family Winery, where he spent nearly a decade helping craft some of Washington State's most sought-after wines under Master of Wine Bob Betz. It was under the guidance and support of Bob and Cathy Betz that Ross and his family started Ross Andrew Winery in 1999. Three barrels became 15, then 30, and now nearly 125 barrels of red wine rest peacefully in the cellar each vintage.

Along the way, Ross has focused his efforts on single parcels of vineyard land: Boushey Vineyards where some of the most unique—and character-filled—clones of syrah can be found; Celilo Vineyard, planted to some of the oldest vines of pinot gris and gewürztraminer in the Northwest; or Force Majeure Vineyards, perched high atop Red Mountain and with some of the most innovative viticultural practices in the state.

Top: Four different clones of syrah grapes come from some of the oldest plantings of the variety in Washington State.
Photograph by Eugene Mickel

Bottom: Syrah grapes harvested from one of the Ross Andrew blocks at Boushey Vineyards.
Photograph by Randolph Mickel

Facing page: The vineyards of Washington State's Columbia Valley produce grapes with incredible depth and concentration while maintaining wonderful finesse and balance.
Photographs by Eugene Mickel

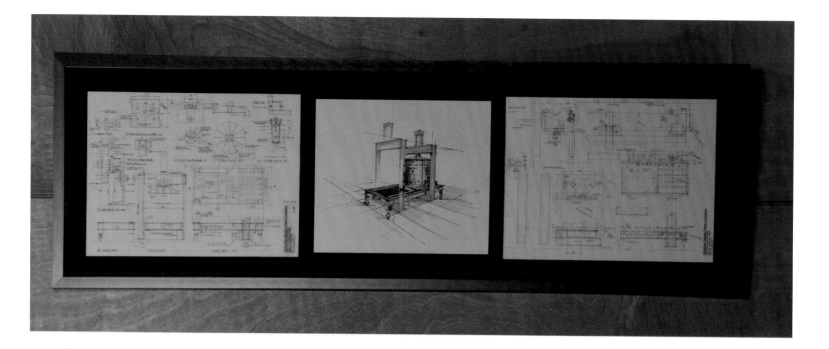

Innovation has also been a driving force at the winery. In early 2004, while still at Betz Family Winery, Ross, his stepfather Ned, and some incredible minds created, designed, and patented the design for a more efficient basket press—an element that has been in existence for more than 1,000 years. Today their basket press is a staple at more than 70 wineries, from Santa Barbara and Napa to Washington.

Ross believes there are still many great discoveries to be made in Washington, both in terms of wine production and viticulture. With a good, long horizon, Ross anticipates being part of a wine community that will continue to build upon the incredible work done over the past 30-plus years. It's the work being done in Washington's great vineyards and cellars that will help anchor Washington State as a benchmark wine-producing region in the minds and glasses of professionals and consumers across the globe.

Above: Drawings of the patented basket press design by Ned Nelson.

Left: The patented basket press designed by Ned is now in use by wineries across the United States and is built by Carleson & Associates in Healdsburg, California.

Facing page: Ross and daughter Lyla at their tasting room in Woodinville.
Photographs by Andréa Johnson

WINE

Meadow Pinot Blanc
Pair with Piatti Restaurant's roasted Alaskan halibut, spring onions, English peas, asparagus, and Limoncello vinaigrette.

Celilo Vineyard Pinot Gris
Delightful with Chez Shea's fresh Washington corn, carrot, and ginger soup.

Boushey Vineyards Syrah
Incredible with Monsoon East's kurobuta pork belly, long-cooked collards, kabocha squash dumplings, and red rice vinegar.

Columbia Valley Cabernet Sauvignon
Succulent with dry-aged beef ribeye, barbecued medium rare, with a side of fingerling potatoes roasted in duck fat.

Tastings
Open to the public Thursday through Sunday

Watch a video of winemaker Ross Mickel discussing a few of his favorite wines served in Ross Andrew Winery's tasting room.

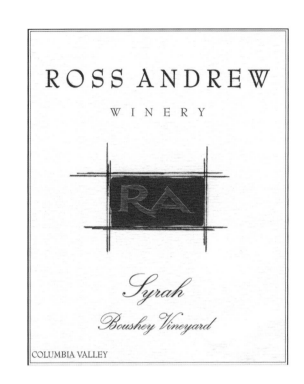

ROSS ANDREW

WINERY

Syrah

Boushey Vineyard

COLUMBIA VALLEY

Soos Creek Wine Cellars

Kent

A passion for the art of winemaking, a background in finance, and a conservative nature: David Larsen, the man who embodies all three, has quietly emerged onto the Washington wine scene as an innately talented winemaker. Today wine drinkers rely on his personal venture, Soos Creek Wine Cellars, to deliver consistently great wine that's eminently drinkable right away and gets even better with age.

At the age of 23, David traveled to Europe and tasted his first glass of truly good wine. Impressed by how it enhanced cuisine, he soon took up winemaking as a serious hobby. At home in Washington, he began making wine from the blackberries on his parents' property. He started at The Boeing Company's finance department in 1975, where he learned the skills essential to running his own business. A trip to Napa Valley with his wife a few years later only deepened his desire to found his own winery, but—risk-conscious—he wasn't sure if Washington was ready. He joined the Boeing Employees' Wine and Beermaking Club in 1987 to begin making grape wine; within a year he was convinced he had a good product and within two he had founded Soos Creek—in his garage.

The name Soos Creek, a nearby creek, was the first suggestion David received when he told friends he'd give a case of wine to the person who named the winery. It was vetted by a marketing firm owned by the man who named Starbucks and the fledging winery was officially christened Soos Creek Wine Cellars. In 1994, David moved to a home with a larger detached garage for winemaking, and in 2008 he built a new home with a dedicated winery building on his property. It's best described as functional, utilizing a low-cost, creative design to stay cool day and night, with radiant heating in the floor to aid fermentation temperatures. Along the way, 2004 saw his departure from Boeing after 28 years in order to focus full-time on winemaking.

Top: Owners Cecile and Dave Larsen sharing a chair at their one-of-a-kind, 50-year-old painted glass dining table

Bottom: Soos Creek's flagship wine, the perennially popular Champoux Vineyard Cabernet Sauvignon

Facing page: Sagemoor Vineyard, a primary source of cabernet sauvignon, cabernet franc, and merlot grapes, overlooking the Columbia River
Photographs by Andréa Johnson

Soos Creek's portfolio is all red—primarily cabernet sauvignon, merlot, and cabernet franc—reflecting David's own preference for Bordeaux wines, and a small amount of syrah for fun. He strives for balanced, delicious flavors with relatively moderate alcohol and good structure for longevity. He believes the most important factor is the vineyard, so he sources grapes from a dozen of the best of the best vineyards in the Columbia Valley appellation. Champoux Vineyard in particular has long been a Soos Creek partner; David's first commercial wine used its fruit and Champoux grapes are known as a Soos Creek specialty today. David lets demand dictate supply and typically sells out of vintages; he's also very cautious about pricing. The result is a measured popularity and preference among Washington enophiles.

Soos Creek is also a family business; David's wife Cecile is vice president, Kevin helps design the labels, and David and Jeff pitch in during their annual open house. The family also collaborates on whimsical names like Sundance and Commander Comet. Above all, Soos Creek wines speak to value, substance, flavor, precision, and considerable winemaking ability.

Left: 2010 vintage wines aging in French oak barrels, 40 percent of which are new each year.

Facing page: Dave and Cecile in the winery with their sons Jeff, Kevin, and David. Not shown are daughters-in-law Carrie and Kari and grandkids Kate and Jack.
Photographs by Andréa Johnson

Champoux Vineyard Cabernet Sauvignon
Pair with filet mignon.

Palisade
(merlot)
Serve with rack of lamb with green mint jelly.

Ciel du Cheval Vineyard Bordeaux Blend
Pair with New York steak.

Artist Series #8
(primarily cabernet franc)
Serve with baked salmon.

Tastings
Open by invitation only, seasonally

Watch a video of owners David and Cecile Larsen discussing their 2008 Champoux Vineyard Bourdeaux blend.

SOOS CREEK
Champoux Vineyard
Horse Heaven Hills Red Wine

Sparkman Cellars
Woodinville

Inspired by the birth of their first daughter, Chris and Kelly Sparkman decided they wanted to have a life focused on their family. With support from their parents, they started Sparkman Cellars in 2004. Chris had served as manager, sommelier, and wine buyer for some of the country's finest restaurants—among them Commander's Palace in New Orleans and Todd English's Olives in Washington, D.C. Kelly, with a background in wildlife biology, left the veterinary field to start the family when their first daughter was born. Together they worked tirelessly to establish their winery while they both simultaneously worked other full-time jobs: Kelly raising the girls, Chris as restaurant general manager. The day their daughter, Stella, entered first grade, Chris resigned as GM to completely focus on their winery and family.

Sparkman Cellars sources fruit from Washington's Columbia Valley, Red Mountain, and Yakima Valley and Oregon's Willamette Valley. Chris and Kelly carefully chose vineyards farmed by some of Washington State's most respected growers, including Boushey, French Creek, Klipsun, Ciel du Cheval, Olsen, and Obelisco in Washington and Temperance Hill Vineyard in Oregon. The winery's portfolio of varietals includes sauvignon blanc, chardonnay, roussanne, cabernet sauvignon, merlot, malbec, pinot noir, petit verdot, and syrah.

Their daughters each have a classic Bordeaux blend named after them, as well. Stella Mae is a cabernet sauvignon-focused blend and Ruby Leigh a merlot dominant blend. Kelly's special project, Pearl Sauvignon Blanc, was named Woodinville's best sauvignon blanc in its first iteration in 2009.

Left: Meticulous sourcing of French cooperage is a hallmark of Sparkman Cellars' commitment to quality, which in turn produces award-winning wines.

Facing page: Fruit sourced from Washington's finest vineyards is a key to Sparkman Cellars' success.
Photographs by Andréa Johnson

Other highly decorated wines include Lumière Chardonnay, Preposterous Malbec, Kingpin Cabernet Sauvignon, and Darkness and Ruckus syrahs. Sparkman Cellars has been named 2010 *Wine Spectator* Rising Star, 2011 *Wine Enthusiast* Cult Winery, and 2011 *Wine & Spirits* Top 100 Winery in the World. In addition to three annual release weekends and various tasting events—like Taste Washington Seattle and the Auction of Washington Wine—guests can visit either of Sparkman's two Woodinville tasting rooms year-round. They also periodically offer entry to their Ring of Fire Wine Club.

Top: The Sparkman family, clockwise from bottom right: Stella, Ruby, Kelly, and Chris.

Bottom and facing page: Feeding Elvis the Press during harvest, one of the steps to producing a selection of fine wines.
Photographs by Andréa Johnson

WINE & FARE

Pearl Sauvignon Blanc
Pairs well with freshly shucked Washington oysters.

Lumière Chardonnay
Delicious with Dungeness crab and lemon butter.

L'Autre Pinot Noir
Impressive with grilled salmon and chanterelle mushrooms.

Kingpin Cabernet Sauvignon
Excellent with rack of lamb with a rosemary-mustard crust.

Tastings
Open to the public Saturday and Sunday, year-round
Also available at Hollywood Hills Wine District Tasting Room

Watch a video of winemaker Chris Sparkman discussing
the family-oriented atmosphere at Sparkman Cellars.

SPARKMAN
CELLARS

Spring Valley Vineyard
Walla Walla

S pread amidst the wheat fields of the Walla Walla Valley, Spring Valley Vineyard represents the epitome of a families-owned ranch. Farmed for five generations by the Corkrum and Derby families, many of whom are featured on the winery's labels, the vineyard and winery bring to mind all of the elements that make a family endeavor great.

Born in 1866, Uriah Corkrum grew up in the Walla Walla Valley, where his family had arrived by wagon train from Illinois. His early start as a wheat farmer in the area was thwarted by the depression in 1893, yet he persevered and purchased the ranch at Spring Valley a few years later, devoting the rest of his life to this unique spot 12 miles northeast of Walla Walla.

Since then, Uriah's descendants have continued his tradition of listening to the land and pushing through challenges to create what is now a flourishing wheat ranch, wine grape vineyard, and winery. The vineyard was first planted in 1993 by Uriah's granddaughter Shari Corkrum Derby and her husband Dean Derby. Their son Devin was the winery's builder and founding winemaker, and the first vintage of Uriah, a merlot-based blend of purely estate-grown fruit, was produced in 1999.

Today winemaker Serge Laville—whose youth and early adulthood in France allowed him to experience and learn from some of the most renowned wine professionals—continues to allow nature to take its course in the winemaking process with minimal, careful intervention including picking, sorting, and punching down the wines gently by hand. As Serge says, "I learned to make wine in France, but I learned to make Spring Valley wine from Devin."

Top: Spring Valley Vineyard's winemaker, Serge Laville.

Bottom: Serge tastes wine in the cellar with Dean Derby and Kate Derby Raymond.

Facing page: Nestled amid the rolling wheat fields of southeast Washington State, Spring Valley Vineyard has been home to the Corkrum and Derby families for over a century.
Photographs by Andréa Johnson

Six highly acclaimed, limited-production red wines round out Spring Valley's collection, all crafted solely from estate-grown fruit and named in honor of family members: Uriah, the merlot-based flagship wine; Frederick, a cabernet sauvignon-based blend named for one of Uriah's sons and Shari's father; Nina Lee, a syrah named for Frederick's wife; Katherine Corkrum, a cabernet franc named after Uriah's wife; Mule Skinner, a merlot that honors the person who cared for and drove the mules in all aspects of farming; and Derby, a cabernet sauvignon bringing the Derby heritage into the series.

The character of the winery itself is something that blends right in with the history of the land and the heritage of the family. Built by Devin inside a machine shed on the ranch, the building's rustic farm style is the perfect setting for the 18-month aging process in predominantly French oak barrels, numerous racking for definition, and the final blending under

Serge's meticulous, insightful direction. Ranch tours, offered by the Corkrum, Derby, and Raymond families by appointment, are a must to understand the true sense of the place. At every turn, the vineyard, winery, and wine itself speak to the connection to the terroir, bringing into memory the hard work put in by generations who were—and continue to be—in love with the land.

Left: First planted in 1993, Spring Valley's estate vineyard has grown to include more than 100 acres.

Right: The unique terroir of Spring Valley contributes to the creation of some of Washington's most acclaimed red wines.

Facing page: Tours of Spring Valley Vineyard and Ranch are available by appointment in the summer months.
Photographs by Andréa Johnson

WINE & FARE

Uriah Red Wine
Excellent with hearty beef stew.

Frederick Red Wine
Superb with herbed beef tenderloin.

Nina Lee Syrah
Delicious with braised lamb shanks.

Tastings
Available at Walla Walla tasting room
Open Thursday through Monday

WALLA WALLA
SPRING VALLEY VINEYARD
WASHINGTON

Stevens Winery

Woodinville

There's nothing better than relaxing with a glass of exquisite wine—except perhaps sipping the wine while chatting with unpretentious winemakers. At Stevens Winery, this scene plays out most weekends in the Woodinville tasting room with owners and winemakers Tim and Paige Stevens. Some of the most knowledgeable yet down-to-earth people, they exude a passion that is as infectious as their wines are distinctive.

Located in Woodinville's warehouse district, the winery was born out of Tim's love of fine wine and artistic inspirations. Naturally, he developed a philosophy that views wine as an art form, an experience that is unique to the individual's palate and preferences. Founded in 2002, Stevens Winery releases wines that receive high ratings vintage after vintage.

Tim has always been drawn to wines that speak about the place where they originate from, and he has used this concept to inform every bottle. Crafted strictly from fruit grown in Yakima Valley, Stevens' wines are produced to maintain the distinct essence evident in the valley's fruit. As the oldest, largest, and most diverse wine growing region in Washington, the valley is known for its intensely flavored fruit, resulting in balanced, complex wines—a perfect match for Stevens' goals.

Not only through close relationships with vineyard partners to ensure quality and consistency in flavor, Tim and Paige also continue to handle the grapes in small lots—1.5-ton tanks—to better manage the process and preserve the character of the valley. They also favor French oak barrels for the aging process.

Top: A sculpture, *The Wine Tiki*, made of used barrel staves.
Photograph by Andréa Johnson

Bottom: Stainless clamps and valves, a few tools of the trade.
Photograph by Andréa Johnson

Facing page: Syrah harvest at Dineen Vineyards in Zillah.
Photograph by Tim Stevens

Bordeaux-style reds comprise the majority of the winery's portfolio. Three that are not to be missed include: BlackTongue Syrah, with its very dry, deep notes; Stevens XY Reserve Cabernet Sauvignon, made from only the juiciest of barrels; and Stevens424, the signature blend so named because Stevens is the 424th winery in the state. For each vintage, Tim uses his creative talent to design black-and-white labels that are worthy of recognition by themselves.

In keeping with the Stevens' laid-back personalities, the atmosphere in the Woodinville tasting room is comfortable and family friendly, whether attending the annual summer barbecue for the release of new wines or casually dropping by on a Saturday for a glass or two.

Top: Winemaker Tim Stevens listening to the wine speak to him.

Bottom: Tim busy at work in the cellar.

Facing page: The tasting room showcasing some of Tim's art that adorns the bottles in dramatic black and white.
Photographs by Andréa Johnson

WINE & FARE

StevensXY Reserve Cabernet Sauvingon
Great with sous vide beef tenderloin with a morel mushroom and red wine reduction.

Stevens424 Red Blend
Delicious with wild boar, homemade gnocchi, and fresh figs with red wine sauce made with the 424.

StevensBlackTongue Syrah
Pair with roasted leg of lamb with rosemary and garlic.

Tastings
Open to the public Saturdays

Swiftwater Cellars
Cle Elum

Nestled in the heart of the Cascade Mountains, Swiftwater Cellars presides over the lush green landscape of gently sloping forested hills near a swift river. The winery sits atop the historic Roslyn Coal Mine No. 9, an important part of the coal rush that occurred with the advent of the Northern Pacific Railroad in 1886. It was here where European-born coal miners made their own wines from huckleberries and blackberries.

Don and Lori Watts, owners of Swiftwater Cellars, were inspired to found their winery in 2007 after travels led them through wineries in Europe, South America, and South Africa. After stumbling onto the current location of the winery, they knew they had found the perfect setting to craft stellar wines that are a compilation of their passions and experience. They opened the winery to the public in 2010.

The family's deep roots in the agricultural business have helped shape the winery's program. Top quality products, excellent service, and innovative marketing were keys to success at Watts Brothers, the frozen food company the Watts family owned, and these same values are an integral part of Swiftwater.

Don and Lori focus Swiftwater's wines in two labels. The upper-tier eponymous label includes Bordeaux varietals from Washington and pinot noir from Oregon, all illustrating the exceptional fruit of the Pacific Northwest's growing regions. Enormous depth, concentration, complexity, and cellar aging are hallmarks of these releases. The flagship red, Proprietary Red, is a rich cabernet sauvignon blended with merlot, cabernet franc, petit verdot, syrah, and malbec, all sourced from the most renowned vineyards in Washington. Swiftwater's pinot noir is a single varietal exclusively from Oregon's Willamette Valley; this wine is the

Top: The sun warms the leaves at Zypher Ridge Vineyard, owned by Don and Lori Watts.

Bottom: One of two Swiftwater Cellars barrel rooms fashioned after the inside of Roslyn Coal Mine No. 9.

Facing page: As dusk begins, the warmth of the fire invites visitors into Swiftwater Cellars.
Photographs by Andréa Johnson

culmination of consulting winemaker Tony Rynders' nearly two decades of experience in the valley. Last but certainly not least under the Swiftwater label is syrah, which provides a velvety yet subtly powerful profile with a long finish.

The house label, No. 9, represents the history of the mine and features Red Wine, a best-of-the-rest Bordeaux-based blend that is fruit-forward with medium body; sémillon, a traditional Bordeaux white blend; and pinot noir, an elegant offering that captures the just-ripened flavors of the Willamette Valley.

In addition to sourcing grapes from top-notch vineyards in Washington and Oregon, the family also owns Zephyr Ridge Vineyard in Washington's Horse Heaven Hills, which the family has been tending since 1994. Tony, who works alongside Swiftwater's resident winemaker Linda Trotta, explains that flexibility in sourcing is important because of the undeniable link between high-quality fruit and fine wine. "We are blending the best of both worlds, combining our estate fruit with other top vineyard sources in Oregon and Washington to showcase what the Pacific Northwest has to offer." During production, the wines undergo a gentle filtration process called crossflow, which makes the wine pure and focused with beautiful aromatics. The wines are placed in barrels to rest for a year and a half before they are bottled, creating a bold flavor profile.

Left: After spending the day in the winery, take a short walk up Tipple Hill and enjoy the sweeping views of Suncadia Resort's Rope Rider golf course, voted best new course of the year in 2011 by *Golf Magazine*.
Photograph by Andréa Johnson

Beyond the No. 9 label's connection to the past, the mine's rich history is felt throughout Swiftwater's facility, from entering through the large wooden doors outfitted with the mine's original pick axes to the coal tipple-influenced architecture, the old photographs, the mining relics, and the barrel rooms, which were designed to resemble old coal mining shafts. Overlooking adjacent Suncadia Resort's Rope Rider golf course, the winery is a beautiful mountain lodge, complete with comfortable leather sofas, chimneys, and European accents in the tasting room. From food and wine tastings to music events, Mardi Gras celebrations, and weddings, the winery is an inviting place.

Left: On any given day, Don Watts can be found mingling with visitors, giving tours of the winery, or simply enjoying a glass of wine with guests in the tasting room.

Above left: The beautiful dining space, surrounded by floor-to-ceiling windows offering a panoramic view of the Cascade Foothills, is ideal for corporate meetings, family gatherings, or intimate rehearsal dinners.

Above right: Guests enjoy drinks beside the 36-foot stone fireplace in the Fireside Lounge, a cozy space complete with massage beams made of reclaimed wood from the Oregon Coast.

Facing page: Proprietors Dan and Lori Watts with winemaker Tony Rynders at a pinot noir vineyard in Oregon's Willamette Valley. Swiftwater Cellars embraces the unique identity of the Pacific Northwest, making wines from both Oregon and Washington.
Photographs by Andréa Johnson

A natural pairing with wine is Swiftwater's delicious fare. Two onsite restaurants, Fireside Lounge and Hoist House, not only showcase Swiftwater wine but also Washington cuisine at its finest. Don is a food veteran, having spent more than 30 years in the food industry; he understands the importance of sourcing local and seasonal ingredients when available. Conveniently, one of the local purveyors for tomatoes happens to be Lori's father, further solidifying the family's dedication to freshness.

At Swiftwater, Don and Lori's original intention has been achieved. It is no doubt a family business, where even the smallest newcomers have an important role; their granddaughter Sofia Grace is often seen welcoming visitors. They offer visitors warm hospitality, making them a part of their family in a beautiful resort setting. They have succeeded in building the ultimate destination winery in perfect complement to magnificent wines.

Top: From left to right: winemaker Tony Rynders, owners Lori Watts and Don Watts, and winemaker Linda Trotta.

Bottom: The candle-lit ambience, grand furnishings, custom-built cabinetry, wrought iron fixtures, and a king's dining table give the impression of stepping into the cellars of an Italian villa.

Facing page: Don and Lori Watts are over the rainbow for their granddaughter, Sophia Grace Watts.
Photographs by Andréa Johnson

No. 9 Pinot Noir
Delectable with grilled salmon or tuna, roasted pork, or fruits and nuts.

No. 9 Chardonnay
Delicious with seafood, chicken, and vegetables from the grill.

Proprietary Red
Delightful with steak and rich dishes.

Pinot Noir
Pair with salmon or trout and mushroom risotto with parmesan cheese.

Tastings
Open to the public Monday through Saturday

SWIFTWATER
C E L L A R S

Tapteil Vineyard Winery

Benton City

Encouraging a growing appreciation for cabernet sauvignon, Larry Pearson—a professional in the fields of education and engineering during the 1970s—decided to escape the city and explore the sources of newly acclaimed vintages while also enjoying the ambience of Washington's countryside. As visits to vineyards became more frequent, so did Larry's interest in robust wines as an "agricultural product of unique character," and what was once a favored pastime quickly became a primary focus.

Larry's methodical and logical nature directed his search for the perfect terroir for cabernet sauvignon. After researching areas most known for producing full-bodied reds, he journeyed to Yakima Valley numerous times in 1983 and 1984. Eventually, such journeys led to the Red Mountain area, not yet identified as its own AVA. A specific property exhibiting all of the sought-after characteristics became the initial part of Tapteil Vineyard in the spring of 1984. The soils within the Red Mountain AVA were dramatically formed by the cataclysmic Missoula Floods of more than 10,000 years ago. Wind-blown soils were deposited on glacial sediments that cover basalt, creating a distinctive terroir. Additionally, the rain shadow effect provided by the Cascade Mountains directly influences the character and quality of the grapes. Armed with knowledge of desired soil type, rainfall, heat units, slope, and grape type, Larry consulted with local vineyard managers and winemakers regarding the best areas for growing his passion. Directed to the end of Sunset Road on Red Mountain, he fell in love with three and a half coveted acres and founded Tapteil Vineyard. Today Tapteil Vineyard Winery covers 30 acres and includes a winery that was bonded in 1999.

Top: Larry and Jane Pearson relaxing in their art-filled tasting room over a glass of Tapteil's flagship cabernet sauvignon.

Bottom: Larry pouring Jane a barrel-thief sample as they taste through the latest vintage in preparation for bottling.

Facing page: Panoramic views of Red Mountain and the surrounding valley, enjoyed by visitors during one of the area's annual 300 days of sun.
Photographs by Andréa Johnson

Affectionately referred to as Tapteilians—a nod to the original Yakima River inhabitants referred to as Tapteilmin—family and friends planted the first cabernet vines in 1985. This tradition, along with many other crush and bottling rituals, continues today thanks to a core assembly of supporters.

Tapteil's winemaker is none other than Larry Pearson; his wife Jane manages tasting room activities and is the creative force behind the winery's artful labels, which begin as her full-size paintings. As one of Washington's boutique wineries—producing 500 cases of wines each year—Tapteil keeps only five percent of its grapes for creating award-winning cabernet sauvignon, merlot, syrah, and riesling varietals; the balance of the prized fruit is made available to other notable wineries throughout Washington and Oregon.

The cozy setting and amazing vineyard views define the Tapteil experience. While the future of this rapidly growing region will bring new wineries and vineyards, the approachable and understated atmosphere of Tapteil will remain true to the intimate experience Larry became enamored with all those years ago.

Left: Argus, a standard poodle who serves as head of reception and security, is a constant companion of the Pearsons.

Right: Looking north to the slope of Red Mountain from the original cabernet sauvignon block planted in 1985.

Facing page: Argus standing guard as the Pearsons, amid lavender and roses on Tapteil's terrace, enjoy the sunset over vineyard views.
Photographs by Andréa Johnson

WINE & FARE

Cabernet Sauvignon
Pair with braised lamb with rosemary and garlic or strip steak with arugula and pesto.

Syrah
Pair with smoky spiced T-bone steak with Chilean sauce or Gouda burgers with grilled onions and pickled peppers.

Argus Bone Dry White
Pair with poached salmon with caper butter sauce.

Tastings
Open to the public Thursday through Sunday, seasonally

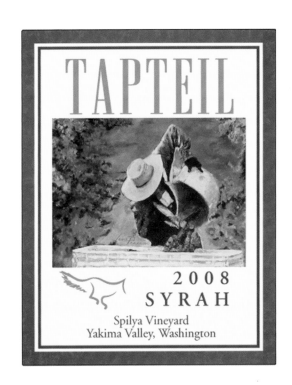

TAPTEIL

2008
SYRAH
Spilya Vineyard
Yakima Valley, Washington

Tenor

Woodinville

No two years at Tenor are ever the same. In fact, those who anxiously await the release of each vintage are always in for a surprise—a much-welcomed surprise. Since its start in 2007, winemaker Aryn Morell has focused on the highest quality wine with no expense spared in its creation. Fate and the year's weather play a large role in determining which fruit will stand out as exceptional at harvest, and only that fruit will eventually make its way into a Tenor bottle.

Applying a very hands-on approach to viticulture and in shaping the wines throughout production, Aryn creates a new experience with each release, which is only offered when it's considered worthy of the Tenor label. One example of his dedication to quality and a completely fresh start with each vintage is the use of new French oak barrels each year, ensuring the purity is controlled from every aspect possible. All of the winery's creations are single varietals with the exception of the 1:1 blend—pronounced one-of-one—yet they all showcase finesse, refinement, power, and grace. A Bordeaux-style blend that references chapter 1 and verse 1 to symbolize new beginnings, 1:1 combines the best fruit from the state's best vineyards, typically including cabernet, merlot, cabernet franc, and malbec.

Aryn likens each Tenor wine to a soloist; it stands alone to tell a story through its music, but it is also a member of a choir, a part of a larger whole. So even though the focus is on single varietals, they are clearly part of the larger viticultural industry that Washington is becoming so well-known for. Just as the greatest wines stand the test of time, Tenor's classically crafted offerings become an investment. Whether five, 10, or 20 years down the road, the wine's presentation will be even greater than the already brilliant vintage enjoyed today.

Top: Tenor features single varietals as well as the esteemed 1:1, a Bordeaux blend.

Middle: The Tenor barrel room showcases the new French oak barrels used to ensure the wine's high quality.

Bottom: Aryn Morell is the winemaker at Tenor.

Facing page: A vineyard in Walla Walla is just one source for Tenor's fine grapes.
Photographs by Andréa Johnson

Tsillan Cellars

Chelan

Tsillan is a Native American word for "deep water." Fifty-five miles long and over 1,500 feet deep, Lake Chelan is framed by mountains rising more than 6,000 feet above the lake. With only 10 inches of annual rainfall, the Chelan Valley has a four-season continental climate characterized by long, hot summers and cold, snowy winters.

When Chelan's famous apple industry fell on difficult times in 2000, Tsillan Cellars owner Dr. Bob Jankelson believed preservation of Chelan's rich agricultural tradition was best served by turning orchards into vinifera vineyards. Confident of the ability to grow world-class wine grapes on these slopes, he then designed and built what is now considered one of Washington State's premier destination wineries.

Inspired by many teaching trips to Italy and love of the Italian lifestyle, Bob designed the winery to resemble an Italian country estate. Natural materials, many imported from Italy, bell and clock towers, Tuscan hues, and the generous use of Italian stone transports visitors to an authentic Tuscan retreat. Three waterfalls cascade into a pool surrounding an island stage connected by stone bridges to the rest of the spectacular landscaped grounds. It has been described as a piece of Tuscany dropped right into the heart of Washington.

Tsillan Cellars is a totally integrated estate winery, allocating virtually all of its 6,000- to 6,500-case production to tasting room visitors and wine club members. General manager Ken Cain capably manages all administrative and hospitality staff. Winemaker Shane Collins works closely with vineyard manager Bal Flores to best express the terroir of Tsillan Cellars vineyards. Special events coordinator Lindsay McKenney oversees a full schedule of weddings, special events, and concerts.

Top: A rainbow over the gates to the Italian-inspired Tsillan Cellars.
Photograph by Andréa Johnson

Bottom: Dr. Bob Jankelson, owner and designer of Tsillan Cellars' vineyards and winery.
Photograph by Andréa Johnson

Facing page: Lily pads in bloom accent one of the spectacular water features that grace the grounds.
Photograph by Martin Bydalek Photography

Gently sloping south-shore vineyards are planted in a north-south direction to maximize airflow and capture the summer heat to assure ripening to perfection. The vineyards have been planted with meticulous attention to detail, even including the hundreds of roses planted at the end of every row of vines. Minimal use of water and chemicals, while gently coaxing the best from this famous agricultural property, produces gold medal-winning wines. The vineyards are presently planted to syrah, merlot, malbec, sangiovese, cabernet sauvignon, cab franc, grenache, nebbiolo, barbera, chardonnay, pinot grigio, riesling, viognier, and gewürztraminer. The hot summer days and cool nights make for the perfect acid/sugar balance. Tsillan Cellars wines have won more than 200 gold, double gold, best-of-varietal, and best-of-show awards in major wine competitions.

Visitors to Tsillan Cellars are assured a complete wine-region experience that includes world-class wine, Italian cuisine, and music to be shared with family and friends. It is Washington State's ultimate la dolce vita wine destination.

Top: The sun rises over an Italian landscape bordering the shores of Lake Chelan.
Photograph by Andréa Johnson

Bottom: World-class dining awaits at Sorrento's Ristorante, complemented by Tsillan Cellars' gold medal-winning wines.
Photograph by Martin Bydalek Photography

Facing page: The grand entry transports visitors to the ultimate food, wine, and music experience.
Photograph by Andréa Johnson

WINE & FARE

Estate Pinot Grigio
Pair with insalata caprese: fresh mozzarella, roma tomatoes, fresh basil, extra virgin olive oil, and balsamic vinegar.

Estate Riesling
Exquisite with an earthy, heavier-style soup, such as wild portabello mushroom bisque.

Estate Sinistra
Delicious with cannelloni Tuscano, which is ricotta, sweet Italian sausage, basil, egg, and spinach wrapped in a pasta sheet with marinara and then baked.

Lakeside Vineyard Bellisima Rossa
Lovely with the flavors of wild game, such as roasted duck served with plum sauce.

Tastings
Open daily, year-round

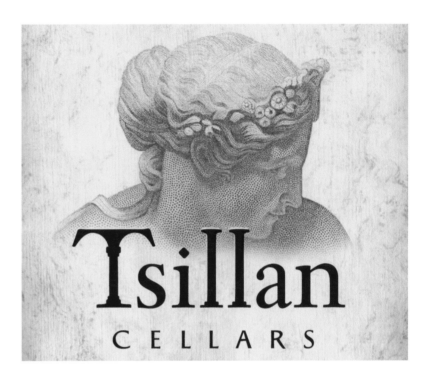

Tunnel Hill Winery

Chelan

Motivated by an economic downturn in the apple industry during the late 1990s, third-generation Sunshine Farms owner Denny Evans started to seek out alternative agricultural ventures. A successful planting of pinot noir in 2001 confirmed Denny's decision to grow European grapes with the intention of making table wine. The vines became a symbol of hope for the Evans family, one that has since come into full fruition.

Formally established in 2004, Tunnel Hill Winery began in a modified carport and has since graduated to a French-inspired, mid-century cottage made from rocks quarried from a nearby tunnel. The cottage is situated on the main road, which leads into the valley, and welcomes thousands of visitors to Lake Chelan and its splendid appellation each year.

As the third-deepest lake in the United States, Lake Chelan's waters can be seen from a bird's-eye view just atop the property's hills, a few hundred yards from the shoreline. A sub-appellation of the vast Columbia Valley AVA, Lake Chelan offers lake-effect benefits—a phenomenon which maintains moderate temperatures, prevents frost damage to vines, and increases hang time for the grapes for complete maturation. Pinot noir flourishes there as a result, with a full-bodied balance that's unmatched; only the estate riesling rivals it in popularity. Other notable varietals include syrah, viognier, cabernet sauvignon, and zinfandel, while malbec is on the horizon.

Top: Guests are greeted with the beautiful stonework that encompasses the buildings and grounds of Tunnel Hill Winery.
Photograph by Andréa Johnson

Bottom: Riesling hangs ripe the morning of harvest.
Photograph by Guy Evans

Facing page: Canadian geese fly south over Lake Chelan and Tunnel Hill estate vineyards.
Photograph by Andréa Johnson

Fourth-generation farmer Guy Evans is a versatile asset. As a winemaker, he draws on an extensive background in agriculture for technique and inner creativity for direction. As a filmmaker, he is responsible for investigating the apple market crisis and creating an Emmy-nominated documentary entitled "Broken Limbs: Apples, Agriculture, and the New American Farmer" in 2004. He's also father to the fifth Lake Chelan Evans generation, continuing with tradition and ensuring the family legacy.

Weaving together the threads of community, agriculture, and fellowship, Tunnel Hill embraces winemaking and farming year-round. Sister business The Sunshine Farm produces organic vegetables as well as a multitude of apples, cherries, and peaches. Several seasonal dinners and estate events offer winery visitors the chance to taste the farm's food and wine products together. With a simple request for guests to "come to your senses," the winery conveys the essence of the vineyard: slow down, relax, and let life bloom.

Top: Tunnel Hill Winery owners Guy and Denny Evans stand in front of the vines.
Photograph by Andréa Johnson

Middle: Winery grounds give way to the Estate Syrah block as late fall sunlight streams across yellowing leaves.
Photograph by Guy Evans

Bottom: Lake Chelan dominates the landscape. From any location, the deep blue lake defines the view.
Photograph by Guy Evans

Facing page: Night falls upon the Tunnel Hill courtyard and main arch.
Photograph by Andréa Johnson

WINE & FARE

Pinot Noir
Pair with barbecued salmon with cucumber yogurt.

Riesling
Pair with capellini pasta primavera made with local, seasonal vegetables.

Syrah
Pair with roasted pork loin and glazed sweet potatoes.

Tastings
Open to the public daily, seasonally

Watch a video of winemaker Guy Evans discussing his passion for and the details of Tunnel Hill wines.

Upland Vineyards

Outlook

Upland Vineyards is located on the slopes of Snipes Mountain in the heart of the Yakima Valley, where the ancient mountain rises unexpectedly from the floor of the valley, paralleling Interstate 82 southwest of Sunnyside. Its elevation protected the area from Glacial Lake Missoula's Ice Age flooding and the resulting cataclysmic events, allowing it to maintain its indigenous alluvial soils. Its position provides ideal sun exposure, creating favorable weather patterns which, at times, protect Upland's crops when crops in other areas are damaged.

A century ago, Snipes Mountain was largely covered with sand and sagebrush. The change to lush farmland occurred gradually and is primarily attributed to the implementation of irrigation and the work of Alfred Newhouse. Understanding Upland Vineyards' present hinges on comprehending its remarkable legacy.

Alfred, born in the shadow of Snipes Mountain in 1923, was the fourth of 10 children. His parents were Dutch immigrants. About eight years before Alfred's birth, his father was one of the pioneers involved in digging the irrigation canals that ultimately crisscrossed the Yakima Valley, changing it from arid land into a farming oasis. William (W.B.) Bridgman, two-term Sunnyside mayor, was instrumental in planning and developing that irrigation system. W.B. had a vision for an irrigated mountain—perfect for wine grapes.

While W.B. was planting wine grapes on Snipes, Alfred was growing up on a family dairy farm—the first in the valley—working alongside his father and six brothers. In 1934, when Alfred was 11, W.B. opened Upland Winery, the first to commercially produce European-style wine in Washington State. W.B. also encouraged Dr. Walt Clore—considered by many

Top: The south slope of Upland Vineyards with Mount Adams in the distance.
Photograph by Andréa Johnson

Left: Steve Newhouse, owner and operator of Upland Vineyards.
Photograph by Mary Jo Newhouse

Facing page: Looking out from Snipes Mountain toward Yakima River.
Photograph by Andréa Johnson

to be the father of Washington wine—to plant vinifera grapes at the Irrigation Experiment Station in Prosser to further the industry and encourage others to plant different varieties.

As the years progressed, Alfred and W.B., each involved with their endeavors, were destined to become intertwined. In 1945, Alfred married Pauline Schilperoort, a daughter of Dutch immigrants. Their seven children were all born and reared in the shadow of Snipes Mountain. By 1966, they had purchased acreage on the mountain, moved their growing family there, and planted a cherry orchard. When the opportunity arose to acquire the land W.B. had planted with grapes, Alfred did not hesitate.

Gradually Alfred and his family expanded on the original plantings, leveling the land and developing orchards and vineyards on the mountain. The expansion continues today and, in honor of the winery that preceded it, is known as Upland Vineyards.

Upland is a family operation. Following in Alfred's footsteps are his surviving son, Steve, and his wife Michelle, three of their sons—Todd, Keith, and Nic—and one of his daughters, Marla. In 2011, Newhouse Family Vineyards released its first label, Vestige, dedicated to Alfred in honor of his influence and impact on the family and the industry.

Above: Through the gully down to the vines.

Right: Nicolaus, Todd, and Keith Newhouse.

Facing page bottom: Driving through the vineyards.
Photographs by Andréa Johnson

Surrounded by the lush growth of cherries, apricots, nectarines, peaches, prunes, pears, apples, and juice and table grapes, row after row of wine grapes can be seen on nearly half of Upland's grounds. Several of the varieties that W.B. planted are now firmly rooted in the rich soils, next to more than 35 varieties of vinifera that make up the vineyards. Today more than 30 wineries throughout the state source grapes from Upland.

Extending his grandfather's vision, Todd and his wife Amber established Upland Estates Winery. In 2007, Todd partnered with soil scientist Joan Davenport to research and petition for federal AVA recognition of the unique area. Two years later, Snipes Mountain AVA was officially designated. Upland Vineyards is located entirely within the AVA.

Upland Vineyards is firmly entrenched on Snipes Mountain. The Newhouse family is dedicated to maintaining and enhancing Alfred's legacy while continually contributing to the success of Washington wines.

Above: Grape harvest.

Left: Marla Newhouse and Newhouse Family Vineyards Vestige.

Facing page: North slope of Upland Vineyards on Snipes Mountain.
Photographs by Andréa Johnson

WINE & FARE

Upland Estates Chardonnay
Pair with pan-seared sea scallops with saffron fennel fish fumet and brown butter.

Upland Estates Malbec
Pair with sautéed beef tenderloin medallions and Argentinean steak.

Upland Estates Teunis
Pair with fines herbes-crusted smoked American wagyu ribeye.

Newhouse Family Vineyards Vestige
Pair with rare elk loin, chanterelle duxelles, and blackcurrant demiglace.

Tastings
Available at Upland Estates Tasting Room, Outlook; Wine O'Clock Wine Bar, Prosser; and Warehouse District, Woodinville

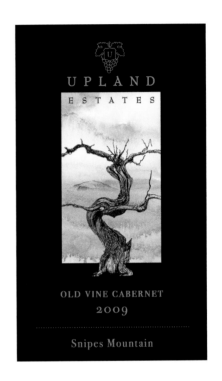

Va Piano Vineyards

Walla Walla

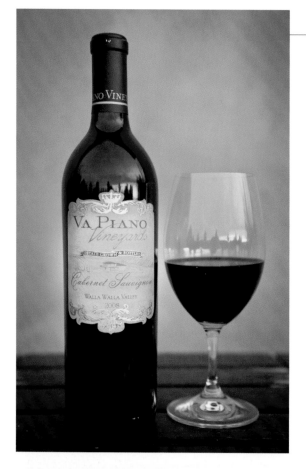

In Italian, "*chi va piano, va sano y va lontano,*" means "he who goes slowly, goes safely and goes far," which perfectly illustrates the Florentine focus on taking time to enjoy the journey. This saying became Justin Wylie's mantra after his collegiate experience in the Italian countryside left an undeniable impression on him. From the grand architecture and religious art to the rich history and alluring landscapes, everything about the area intrigued Justin. Modeled brilliantly by an Italian professor, Bruno Segatta—who has become Justin's informal mentor—the Italian culture became part and parcel of Justin's philosophies.

Justin was understandably charmed by the family-oriented culture and the hospitable nature of Italians, much of which centered on good food and wine. But he could not leave them as memories and began to find ways to make them live again in Washington, his homeland and his family's place of residence for four generations.

He began meagerly, experimenting with wine blends in his garage and termed his test lots Vino del Garage wines. Five years, countless viticulture and enology classes, and a small cult following later, Justin planted Va Piano Vineyards in 1999 with his own hands. Formerly planted in wheat, the 20-acre estate is located in the southeast corner of the Walla Walla Valley. Known for red varietals such as cabernet sauvignon, syrah, merlot, cabernet franc, and petit verdot, Va Piano Vineyards embodies the definition of high-quality fruit. A viticulturist first, Justin established the quality of his grapes before opening the winery in 2005.

Top: The 2008 Estate Cabernet Sauvignon is a classic example of what Washington State has to offer.

Bottom: Justin Wylie is Va Piano Vineyards' owner and winemaker.

Facing page: Va Piano's Tuscan-inspired tasting room is simply stunning, especially at sunset.
Photographs by Andréa Johnson

The Tuscan-inspired tasting room that can be visited today is now the host of Justin's hospitable dream and the Italian culture. Here guests enjoy his variety of wines, such as Bruno's Blend, named in honor of the mentor himself. Patrons are made to feel like family at Va Piano Vineyards as impromptu plates of paninis are often passed around by Liz, Justin's wife, while their three children, Jake, Arianna, and Sienna, can often be spotted playing on the vast property.

Top: Artwork by Father Bruno Segatta decorates the inside of the tasting room.

Middle left: The row marker identifies just one row of many that cover the 20-acre estate.

Middle right: The Wylie family includes Justin, Liz, Jake, Arianna, and Sienna.

Bottom: Va Piano is located south of beautiful Walla Walla.

Facing page: Va Piano sits on gorgeous rolling hills with an extraordinary view of the Blue Mountains.
Photographs by Andréa Johnson

Cabernet Sauvignon
Pair with grilled hanger steak with bacon chimichurri.

Syrah
Serve with braised lamb shanks in port sauce.

Merlot
Couple with ribeye steak topped with gorgonzola butter.

Tastings
Open to the public daily, seasonally

Walla Walla Vintners
Walla Walla

Gordy Venneri and Myles Anderson are firm believers that doing what you love and following your passion pays off in numerous ways. As owners and winemakers at Walla Walla Vintners, they began making wine as a hobby after Gordy visited family members in southern Italy who crafted homemade wines for personal enjoyment. He loved how they created wines to share with friends and family, allowing the entire process to be part of their lifestyle.

Gordy and Myles started in 1981 as hobbyists, crafting red wines for themselves, family, and friends. That creative journey allowed them to really understand the process, practicing winemaking and learning from their mistakes, all while indulging their passion. By 1995, they made the leap to sell their wines commercially—becoming just the eighth winery in Walla Walla. Their skill for making outstanding red wines has taken them from a first production of 500 cases to more than 5,000 cases annually today.

The key to their success is obviously their enjoyment of what they do. In the winery's magnificent setting in the shadow of the Blue Mountains, every wine Gordy and Myles bottle is an expression of heart, soul, and passion. With Gordy's Italian heritage, it was only natural that they follow traditional, labor-intensive winemaking techniques, including frequently tasting the fruit before harvesting, sorting and picking by hand, manually punching down the grapes in open-top fermenters, and hand-racking each barrel four times a year. Gordy's roots also led him to become one of the first Washington wineries to produce an acclaimed sangiovese, along with a stunning blend, Bello Rosso.

Left: Owners Gordy Venneri and Myles Anderson with their wines and enjoying a tasting.

Facing page: The magnificent view from atop the hill north of Walla Walla Vintners.
Photographs by Andréa Johnson

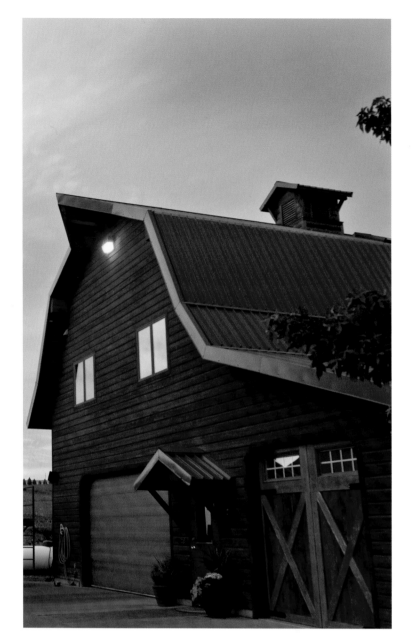

Walla Walla Vintners prides itself on producing only red wines and in limited quantities. That focus has resulted in an outstanding cabernet franc. Traditionally a blending grape in France, the fruit grows so well in Washington that it can easily stand alone. This inherent quality pairs well with Gordy and Myles' techniques—so well in fact that *Seattle* magazine has declared their cab franc the best in the state for numerous years in a row.

Their other wines, which receive acclaim for their superb quality, consistency, and reasonable prices, include: cabernet sauvignon, malbec, merlot, sangiovese, syrah, and specially crafted Bordeaux blends. All of the fruit is sourced from the best sustainable vineyards in the Walla Walla and Columbia valleys. A new estate vineyard, which was planted in 2008 with 11 acres of certified grape stock, is showing incredible promise.

When visitors arrive at one of the most picturesque wineries in America they are often met by Myles or Gordy and welcomed into the tasting room. Visiting with customers and sharing in wine tastings—which are always free—is their favorite part of the job. It's in those times that Myles and Gordy see their creations enjoyed and appreciated, and where others get a true taste of the passion that goes into every bottle of Walla Walla Vintners wine.

Above left: The iconic red barn at Walla Walla Vintners.

Top: From left to right, the Walla Walla Vintners crew: Myles Anderson, Judah Pira, William vonMetzger, Gordy Venneri, and Todd Bernave.

Bottom: Estate vineyard grapes ready for harvest.

Facing page: The pastoral setting under the shade trees of the picnic area next to the wood-fired oven.
Photographs by Andréa Johnson

Columbia Valley Cabernet Franc
Wonderful with roasted wild salmon on cedar plank and a side of scalloped potatoes, heavy cream, Gruyère cheese, and nutmeg.

Walla Walla Valley Merlot
Perfect with roasted meat such as rack of lamb.

Columbia Valley Bello Rosso
Excellent with Italian tuna in olive oil, chopped garlic, parsley, and anchovy simmered in San Marzano crushed tomatoes and tossed with buttered rigatoni.

Walla Walla Valley Malbec
Delicious with dessert, especially loganberry spread on pâte sucrée or cookie dough.

Tastings
Open Fridays and Saturdays, or by appointment

Waterbrook Winery

Walla Walla

Quintessential to Washington's young wine country, Waterbrook Winery was founded in 1984 and was the fourth bonded winery in Walla Walla's now-thriving wine community. As one of the anchors in Washington's agricultural phenomenon, the winery has maintained a position of leadership among its peers for over two decades. Primarily recognized for producing affordable wines of Columbia Valley class, the winery has created a multitude of 90-plus point vintages according to *Wine Spectator*, and twice as many have been deemed a best buy by *Wine Enthusiast*. Selections from four tiers of wines—value, mélange, reserve, and Meritage—have received amorous attention from the media, connoisseurs, and everyday consumers.

According to experts, superior fruit is the foundation of all good wine. Waterbrook uses grapes harvested from Columbia Valley as critical building blocks for creating well-rounded wines of dynamic nature. After harvest, grapes are left to the winemaker for complete transformation into a luscious vintage.

Born in San Francisco and raised in Napa Valley, John Freeman was immersed in a culture of fine wine from a young age. As a resident of California's famed wine country, John began his career in his home state and spent 12 years working diligently there until 2002. After being exposed to the wide array of blends coming out of Washington, he felt compelled to contribute to the region's still-developing industry. In January of 2003, he began as Waterbrook's assistant winemaker and was promoted to winemaker just two years later. His passion is noticeable in every complex and refined wine that consumers uncork. His eagerness to learn and ability to solve problems are maximized at the winery's new facility, fully equipped with the latest technology to optimize production and raise quality standards.

Top: Winemaker John Freeman.
Photograph courtesy of Waterbrook Winery

Bottom: Canyon Ranch Vineyard in the Columbia Valley.
Photograph by Andréa Johnson

Facing page: Waterbrook Winery.
Photograph by Andréa Johnson

The new state-of-the-art facility was constructed in 2008 and contains a staggering 10,000 barrels for aging, 60-plus steel tanks, and an industrial bottling line. Its wow factor is matched by the contemporary tasting room, which offers panoramic views of the Northwest's natural beauty from floor-to-ceiling windows. Well-manicured grounds and the grand Blue Mountains can be experienced fully from an inviting patio and seating area for those who wish to venture outside.

Above: Waterbrook tasting room.
Photograph by Andréa Johnson

Left: Three of Waterbrook's varietals.
Photograph courtesy of Waterbrook Winery

Facing page: The patio at the tasting room.
Photograph by Andréa Johnson

WINE & FARE

Meritage
(40% cabernet franc, 23% merlot, 15% cabernet sauvignon, 12% petit verdot, 10% malbec)
Pair with roasted beef tenderloin stuffed with sundried tomatoes and pine nuts.

Mélange Noir
(20% syrah, 19% sangiovese, 12% merlot, 11% cabernet sauvignon, 11% malbec, 7% tempranillo, 7% grenache, 13% other red varietals)
Drink with filet mignon smothered in a red wine reduction sauce flavored with shallots, garlic, and thyme.

Reserve Cabernet Sauvignon
(88% cabernet sauvignon, 10% cabernet franc, 2% malbec)
Try with rosemary braised lamb shanks simmered in a cabernet sauvignon-based broth.

Chardonnay
(100% chardonnay)
Sip with salmon grilled on an untreated cedar plank dressed with pepper and honey.

Tastings
Open to the public daily, year-round

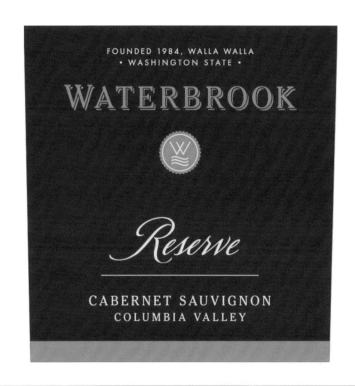

Willow Crest Winery

Prosser

Dave Minick first planted wine grapes on his family farm in 1982 with the intention of selling them. By 1995, his hard work had paid off as a small vineyard of riesling, gewürztraminer, chardonnay, cabernet sauvignon, and merlot flourished in the cool atmosphere and dynamic soil. Because of increasing product demands and current success, Dave added syrah, cabernet franc, and pinot gris the following year. As his first-rate grapes were being purchased by prime wineries, Dave realized his own desire to make wine and further expanded his operation. By 2002, he added Rhône varietals and increased select varietals. Today the family vineyard includes 185 acres of grapes—some of which are still sold to neighboring winemakers—and he now reserves most of the varietals for making crisp pinot gris, mouthwatering riesling and bold syrah at the estate's new high-tech facility.

Willow Crest Winery is home to a Tuscan-inspired tasting room that is warm and inviting. Located in Prosser, the tasting room is fittingly situated on Merlot Drive in the town's charming wine village. Warm-weather festivities welcome tasters outside to socialize or sit back on the spacious patio.

Top: Winery founder Dave Minick.
Photograph courtesy of Willow Crest Winery

Bottom: Event tasting in the barrel room.
Photograph by Andréa Johnson

Facing page: Willow Crest estate vineyard.
Photograph by Andréa Johnson

The Woodhouse
Wine Estates
Woodinville

B ijal Shah, owner of The Woodhouse Wine Estates, has been a passionate wine collector and enthusiast for as long as he can remember. His foray into winemaking can be traced back to his time in the fashion industry, entertaining clients with good wines. Bijal reached out to his uncle, Tom Campbell, a former owner of Horizon's Edge Winery and one of the first vintners in Washington to plant malbec and Bordeaux varietals. He asked Tom to produce 100 cases of wine for him to serve at dinners and sell to friends. When the cases sold out quickly, Bijal realized that he could turn his passion for wine into a profession.

In 2004, Bijal and his wife, Sinead, opened the winery in partnership with Tom, naming it The Woodhouse Wine Estates. The vision was a boutique winery passionate about crafting high-quality, complex, and age-worthy red wines. Numerous accolades through the years are proof that they have certainly achieved their vision.

For Bijal, owning a winery allows him to focus on three of his favorite things: food, wine, and people. With the help of Tom and Woodhouse head winemaker Jean-Claude Beck, Bijal delivers Old World-style, terroir-driven wines. Relying on Tom's connection and experience with Washington terroir, Woodhouse sources its grapes from mature vineyards which Tom planted or provided consulting services for. Typically releasing the wines later than most wineries allows full integration and expression of flavor.

Top: Winemaker Jean-Claude Beck and owner Bijal Shah outside the Woodhouse barrel room.
Photograph by Andréa Johnson

Bottom: Three of the premium labels produced by Woodhouse.
Photograph by Steve Schneider

Facing page: The impressive chandeliers in the cellar.
Photograph by Andréa Johnson

While some of the winery's portfolio is readily available, reserve and low production wines are aged in new oak barrels and can only be found at the winery's tasting room, a warm, spacious building in the heart of Woodinville. Woodhouse produces many Old World varietals, including cabernet sauvignon, cabernet franc, and merlot. Uniquely, Woodhouse releases its wines under five labels, two of which are named after the Shahs' children, Kennedy and Hudson. The Maghee and Dussek labels are named after close family friends, and Darighe, Gaelic for "red," is a nod to Sinead's Irish background and her red hair.

As a boutique winery, many of Woodhouse's wines sell out within a few weeks of being released. While Bijal hopes they will continue to increase production throughout the years, he firmly believes that making wine is about enjoying how a wine feels and understanding how it works, not the amount of wine produced or attaining reviews. He likens wine to a symphony, and like a good conductor, he takes the wine through every note to deliver the best performance.

Top: Barrel after barrel of premium wine.
Photograph by Steve Schneider

Middle: Woodhouse is the perfect setting for a special event.
Photograph by Jonathan Schmidt

Bottom: Owners Bijal and Sinead Shah inside the tasting room.
Photograph by Andréa Johnson

Facing page: The Kennedy Shah Reserve wines, created exclusively for the wine club and Woodinville tasting room.
Photograph by Steve Schneider

WINE & FARE

Darighe
Pair with New York strip steak, roasted potatoes, and green beans.

Dussek Cabernet Sauvignon
Delightful with paella.

Kennedy Shah Reserve
Incredible with smoked salmon.

Hudson Shah Viognier
Delicious with shrimp curry or Singapore noodles.

Tastings
Open to the public Monday through Saturday

Watch a video of the winemaker discussing the complementary natures of riesling and cabernet sauvignon.

The **Woodhouse**
WINE ESTATES

Woodward Canyon

Walla Walla Valley

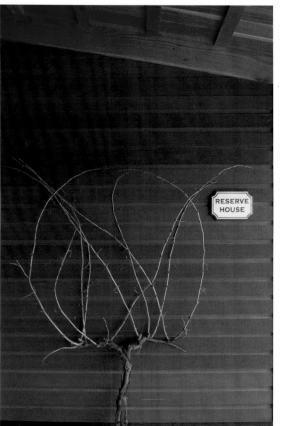

Before being green was fashionable and sustainability was socially strived for, Rick Small and his wife Darcey Fugman-Small were redefining the Walla Walla Valley wine scene bottle by bottle, cork by cork. Beyond being members of the local wine alliance and serving as board members on various wine industry and charitable committees, the Smalls maintain a high standard for their own winemaking operation, practicing cork, glass, and cardboard recycling and participating in a variety of eco-friendly organizations—all while delivering prized wines.

Affectionately referred to by friends and team members as Woody, Woodward Canyon was the second winery established in the Walla Walla Valley appellation—within the larger Columbia Valley AVA—and is located in the community of Lowden, 13 miles west of Walla Walla. Just three miles north of the winery, at an elevation of nearly 900 feet, is the estate vineyard. First planted in 1977 amid family-owned wheat fields, it has grown into 42 impressive acres of cabernet sauvignon, merlot, cabernet franc, chardonnay, and sauvignon blanc, along with trial varieties of northern Italian and Rhône assortments. The soils in this region are comprised of windblown loess over flood silts and fractured basalt, and average yields are typically in the two-and-a-half tons per acre range, depending upon growing season, variety, and clone. Woodward Canyon is also a partner in the renowned Champoux Vineyard, located in the Horse Heaven Hills appellation.

Top: Woodward Canyon is owned by Rick Small and Darcey Fugman-Small.
Photograph by Colby D. Kuschatka

Bottom: Woodward Canyon's Reserve House is powered by solar panels and a high-efficiency heating and cooling system.
Photograph by Andréa Johnson

Facing page: Rick is the third generation in his family to farm the land where the estate vineyard was planted in 1976.
Photograph by Colby D. Kuschatka

For third-generation farmer Rick, who is degreed in agriculture, interest in wine began during a post-collegiate trip abroad and grew during visits to the California wine country. Rick learned to make wine by reading, applying techniques, and evolving his strategy based on results. In 2003, Rick added Kevin Mott to the Woody family as lead winemaker in order to focus more fully on the care and further development of the vineyard.

In 1979, Rick met Darcey Fugman, a professional planner for Walla Walla County. A budding lover of wine, Darcey enjoyed bottling homemade chardonnay in Rick's basement during their second date. According to her, "the die was cast" and they were soon married. In 1981, the Smalls founded Woodward Canyon and Darcey has since taken on a pro-active role in the development of the winery and also assisted in garnering recognition of Walla Walla as its own appellation.

Above left: In 1992, the Artist Series cabernet sauvignon was launched, primarily featuring artists from the Pacific Northwest. The artists' works are also featured in the tasting room.
Photograph by Colby D. Kuschatka

Above right: Juan Esparza, vineyard and garden manager, holds tomatoes grown near the vineyard that will be served by a Walla Walla restaurant later that evening.
Photograph by Colby D. Kuschatka

Facing page: An 1870s farmhouse surrounded by perennial gardens serves as the tasting room. Sculptures dot the lawn where picnickers are welcome.
Photograph by Colby D. Kuschatka

These days the winery and vineyard are doing quite well, earning the attention of wine aficionados as well as placing five wines—including Washington's first wine listed—on *Wine Spectator*'s Top 100 list and eight wines on *Wine Enthusiast*'s Best of the Year list. After a two-year process, the vineyard is now certified sustainable and harvests organic fruit—uncertified for now. It is also a Salmon-Safe property as specified by the nonprofit organization Low Input Viticulture & Enology and the International Organization for Biological Control. Woodward Canyon uses green materials and energy-saving features throughout the vineyard and on the winery grounds and is well on its way to becoming a Walla Walla County Green Seal business.

In the future, Rick and Darcey would love to develop the culinary side of their business by utilizing the organic vegetable gardens at the vineyard, the produce from which is now sold to local restaurants. Whether wandering through the perennial gardens or touring the renovated 1870s farmhouse-turned-tasting room, guests are sure to experience hospitality intentional to each of the senses.

Top: The Dedication Series/Old Vines cabernet sauvignon, which was begun in 1981, is shown in the Reserve House Library Cellar.
Photograph by Colby D. Kuschatka

Above: Private tastings by appointment are held in the airy Reserve House.
Photograph by Andréa Johnson

Facing page: The Woodward Canyon estate vineyard, located at the west end of the Walla Walla Valley appellation, is certified sustainable and Salmon-Safe.
Photograph by Colby D. Kuschatka

Estate Sauvignon Blanc
Pair with Dungeness crab cakes dipped in lemongrass butter sauce with garlic sautéed asparagus.

Old Vines Cabernet Sauvignon
Pair with Pyrenees sheep milk cheese and raspberry preserves spread across French baguettes.

Merlot
Pair with grapewood smoked Copper River salmon with wild long-grain rice.

Tastings
Open to the public daily, year-round

Watch a video of Rick Small discussing Woodward Canyon's history.

WOODWARD CANYON

Boushey Vineyards, page 276

Klipsun Vineyards, page 281

Sagemoor Vineyards, page 283

Ciel du Cheval Vineyard, page 278

THE VINE

Boushey Vineyards

Grandview

Within Washington State, there's probably no one more in tune with the terroir of the Yakima Valley than Dick Boushey, owner and manager of Boushey Vineyards. And it's obvious to see why. His years of experience—he planted his first grapes in the area in 1976—and his passion for viticulture are difficult to surpass.

Dick was originally a cherry and apple grower, but was intrigued by vitis vinifera after meeting Dr. Walter J. Clore, a pioneer of Washington wine. After experimenting for a few years around his home, Dick planted his first commercial vineyard in 1980 with cabernet sauvignon and merlot, nearly three years before the Yakima Valley was even recognized as a viticultural area. Dick's obsession with the area's potential is explained in the Yakima Valley's cool temperatures that enable the grapes to be harvested a few weeks later, adding complexity to the flavors without over-ripening.

Since Boushey Vineyard's founding, Dick has grown the estate into 125 acres with nearly two dozen grape varieties, and has numerous awards and accolades to certify his success. Using a minimalist approach, Dick manages the vineyards in close collaboration with the winemakers who will use his grapes. A home winemaker himself, he connects with the wineries and understands what they're looking for, giving them the ability to source grapes according to their specifications. The results lead to fruit that produces some of the most critically acclaimed Washington wines.

Top: A syrah block planted in 1993 overlooks the town of Grandview in the Yakima Valley.
Photograph by Glen Holden

Middle: Newly picked cabernet sauvignon.
Photograph by Andréa Johnson

Bottom: Dick and Luanne Boushey with Cooper.
Photograph by Andréa Johnson

Facing page: Spring growth in Boushey Vineyards, looking south toward Grandview and the Horse Heaven Hills.
Photograph by Glen Holden

Ciel du Cheval Vineyard

Red Mountain

Meaning "horse heaven" in French, Ciel du Cheval is the fittingly appointed name for 120 acres of southern-facing terrain overlooking the Horse Heaven Hills. A part of the Red Mountain AVA, the vineyard was purchased in 1991 by business partners and Kiona Vineyards and Winery owners Jim Holmes and John Williams. With two decades' worth of industry-leading experience, the partners further developed the existing estate into an outstanding resource for Washington's premier wineries. Along with averaging 93 points for 2008 vintages, Ciel's grapes are best known for outstanding Bordeaux blends and exceptional syrah. With a fierce concentration on twelve varietals—the most sought-after, like cabernet franc, cabernet sauvignon, syrah, and sangiovese, having multiple clones—outstanding quality has come to be expected.

An ambitious wine collector, Jim's inspiration to grow his own grapes came in 1974 after agricultural research—conducted at a nearby university—proved Washington's climate and terroir ideal for raising grapes. One purchase of land and 10 acres of test lots later, Jim had his first harvest and his life's purpose clarified. In 1994, he became sole proprietor of Ciel du Cheval as long-time business partner John Williams took possession of their first venture, Kiona Vineyards and Winery.

Top: Jim Holmes, owner of Ciel du Cheval Vineyard, checking vineyard irrigation.

Bottom: Cabernet sauvignon grapes approaching harvest.

Facing page: Ciel du Cheval Vineyard's operations center.
Photographs by Andréa Johnson

Klipsun Vineyards

West Richland

Most everyone in the wine industry will admit that good fruit is a requirement for crafting good wine, and likewise good soil and terroir are necessary to grow good fruit. At Klipsun Vineyards, all of these elements come into play, and you would be hard-pressed to find anyone in the Washington wine industry who disagrees.

Planted by husband-wife duo David and Patricia Gelles in 1984, the vineyards at Klipsun—named after the Chinook word for "sunset"—are made up of about 120 acres of mostly merlot and cabernet, with some sauvignon blanc, syrah, sémillon, and nebbiolo. Designed around the philosophy that they only wanted to plant what they would prefer to drink, David and Patricia have certainly taken advantage of the perfect site to create fruit with terrific concentration and depth. And those from far and wide have taken notice, including Quilceda Creek Vintners, Seven Hills Winery, L'Ecole N° 41, EFESTE, Apolloni Vineyards, and Andrew Rich Wines.

As lively as her fuchsia hair color, Patricia energetically emphasizes that her favorite part of the process is meeting the winemakers, from those who are completely new to the business to those who have helped the Washington wine industry become what it is today.

Hardly content to just be satisfied with the status quo, David and Patricia are continually working to enhance the quality of their fruit as well as exploring new opportunities. In recent years, their daughter has even begun to craft her own sémillon with the moniker eKlipse, using fruit from Klipsun. Considering the family's past, you certainly want to pay attention to whatever they choose to do in the future.

Right: Long-time employees Jesus Godinez, Erika Espindola, and Francisco Espindola help harvest the grapes.

Facing page: World class, award-winning, 1984-planted cabernet vines.
Photographs by Andréa Johnson

Sagemoor Vineyards

Pasco

A vineyard original to Washington's wine industry infancy, Sagemoor Vineyards was planted in the late '60s and early '70s over four divided properties including Sagemoor Farms, Bacchus Vineyards, Dionysus Vineyards, and Weinbau Vineyards. Situated in the Columbia Valley AVA, Sagemoor, Bacchus, and Dionysus are positioned near Pasco on southwest-facing hills peering into the Columbia River, while Weinbau has a view of the river near Mattawa in the sub-AVA of Wahluke Slope.

Initially the dream of Albert Ravenholt, Alec Bayless, Syd Abrams, and Winslow Wright, the vineyards barely survived in the beginning due to harsh winters, compromised vines, and poor varietal choices. But the founders' resolve proved strong as they planted and replanted for five years until finally reaching full production. With a combined grape planting of 466 acres, Sagemoor became the only significant vineyard in Washington that could appeal to multiple wineries.

Today the group estate—totaling over 900 acres—provides viniferous varietals to more than 75 wineries under the guidance of managing director John Vitalich, general manager Kent Waliser, and their team of vineyard and production managers, including Derek Way, Servando Rodriguez, and Miguel Rodriguez. A couple of property favorites are cabernet and white riesling.

Top: General manager Kent Waliser and vineyard manager Derek Way together operate the venerable vineyards of Sagemoor, Bacchus, Dionysus, and Weinbau.

Middle: Cabernet sauvignon fruit from Bacchus 9, planted in 1972, is highly sought after for its old vine character. Sagemoor has more than 60 acres of cabernet that was planted in 1972.

Bottom: New white riesling clones coming into production provide opportunities for wineries to create vineyard-designated, world-class riesling that showcases the terroir and climate of Washington.

Facing page: The Bacchus vineyard site, which faces west overlooking the Columbia River, has produced Washington grapes since 1972.
Photographs by Andréa Johnson

INDEX

SPECTACULAR WINERIES

WASHINGTON TEAM

ASSOCIATE PUBLISHER: John Ovesen

ART DIRECTOR: Emily A. Kattan

EDITOR: Jennifer Nelson

PRODUCTION COORDINATOR: London Nielsen

HEADQUARTERS TEAM

PUBLISHER: Brian G. Carabet

PUBLISHER: Jolie M. Carpenter

GRAPHIC DESIGNER: Lilian Oliveira

GRAPHIC DESIGNER: Paul Strength

MANAGING EDITOR: Lindsey Wilson

SENIOR EDITOR: Sarah Tangney

EDITOR: Alicia Berger

EDITOR: Sarah Reiss

EDITOR: Megan Winkler

MANAGING PRODUCTION COORDINATOR: Kristy Randall

PROJECT COORDINATOR: Jessica Adams

PROJECT COORDINATOR: Laura Greenwood

TRAFFIC SUPERVISOR: Drea Williams

DEVELOPMENT & DISTRIBUTION SPECIALIST: Rosalie Z. Wilson

ADMINISTRATIVE COORDINATOR: Amanda Mathers

ADMINISTRATIVE ASSISTANT: Aubrey Grunewald

SIGNATURE PUBLISHING GROUP
CORPORATE HEADQUARTERS
1424 Gables Court
Plano, TX 75075
469.246.6060
www.panache.com